MW00772482

THE
SNUBBY
REVOLVER

The ECQ, Backup, and Concealed Carry Standard

Ed Lovette

Paladin Press • Boulder, Colorado

The Snubby Revolver:
The ECQ, Backup, and Concealed Carry Standard
by Ed Lovette

ISBN 10: 1-58160-382-7
ISBN 13: 978-1-58160-382-8

Printed in the United States of America

Published by Paladin Press, a division of
Paladin Enterprises, Inc.
Gunbarrel Tech Center
7077 Winchester Circle
Boulder, Colorado 80301 USA
+1.303.443.7250

Direct inquiries and/or orders to the above address.

PALADIN, PALADIN PRESS, and the "horse head" design
are trademarks belonging to Paladin Enterprises and
registered in United States Patent and Trademark Office.

Cover photo by Michael Janich.

All other photos by Officer David E. Marcinik,
DUI enforcement specialist with Palm Bay Police Department,
Palm Bay, Florida.

Cover photo: One of the premier examples of the snubby revolver breed is this "Fitz
Special," a .45 Colt New Service revolver customized by the legendary J.H.
FitzGerald for the late Col. Rex Applegate. Colonel Applegate carried this rare
revolver instead of his official sidearm throughout World War II and as a personal
defense weapon for many years after the war. (Photo courtesy of Michael Janich)

Visit our Web site at www.paladin-press.com

Contents

Foreword

THE SUBJECT OF THE short-barreled, or snubby, revolver is unwisely overlooked by many people who are otherwise well prepared to deal with criminal attacks. The self-loading pistol, even with all of its advantages (particularly in the more recent compact models), still cannot match the ratio of power to size and weight the snubby offers.

Particularly when unusual concealment requirements exist, the snub-nose revolver will often be the best armament available. With its rounded lines, the small revolver just doesn't show through a concealing garment or pocket as severely as a pistol does. As pistols are scaled down to approach the snubby's level of compactness, the grip surface area of the weapon is often severely compromised. In order for a pistol to be more concealable than the five-shot snubby, it must be chambered for a cartridge proven to come up short in terms of effectiveness. In short, for very discreet carry or for use as a second to a larger belt gun, the snubby is the standard of comparison, and for good reason: it is very difficult to beat in those applications. I predict that, in this form, the revolver will continue to be used by professionals in the field for the foreseeable future.

For those of you who are instructors, recognizing this is critical. If your student is most likely going to be using a snubby, then revolver technique should be taught with that type of weapon. At least three of the fundamental skills of shooting are affected by switching to a small revolver from a larger handgun. Loading techniques, in particular, should be chosen to maximize the effectiveness of the short extractor rod that accompanies the short barrel. In addition, sight radius is shorter with the snubby than with other handguns, making proper instruction in that area more critical. (Sight movement appears to be extreme due to the short sight radius, which increases the temptation to jerk the trigger as the front sight crosses the target.) The gripping technique must also be adjusted on the smaller guns, particularly for students with large hands.

Using the snub-nose revolver to its full potential is a challenge, but one that is well worth mastering. Ed's book will give you a head start down that path.

—Bert DuVernay
Director, Smith & Wesson Academy
Springfield, Massachusetts

Acknowledgments and Disclaimers

I WOULD LIKE TO THANK Harry Kane, editor of *Combat Handguns*, for permission to use material that was previously printed in my "Survival Savvy" column.

• • •

In accordance with the policy of Central Intelligence Agency (CIA), which requires its employees, past and present, to submit specific types of written material to it prior to publication, a copy of the manuscript for this book was sent to the agency's Publication Review Board. It asked that I include the following disclaimer:

The CIA's Publications Review Board has reviewed the manuscript for this book to assist the author in eliminating classified information, and poses no security objection to its publication. This review, however, should not be construed as an official release of information, confirmation of its accuracy, or endorsement of the author's views.

WARNING

Firearms are potentially dangerous and must be handled responsibly by trainees and experienced shooters alike. The technical information presented here on firearms handling, training, and shooting inevitably reflects the author's beliefs and experience with particular firearms and training techniques under specific circumstances that the reader cannot duplicate exactly. Therefore, the information in this book is presented *for academic study only* and should be approached with great caution. This book is not intended to serve as a replacement for professional instruction under a qualified instructor. It is the reader's responsibility to research and comply with all local, state, and federal laws pertaining to concealed firearms carry and the legal use of a firearm in self-defense.

Introduction

WHY IN THE WORLD would anyone in his right mind choose to write a book today on the snubby revolver? Good question. If we can just skip over the right mind part for now (the jury's still out on that one!), I have to say that I wrote it because it seems to me we're slowly losing all that good revolver "how-to" we learned the hard way over a good many years, often at great risk, sometimes paying the ultimate price. I am concerned that the requisite revolver skills are not being passed on to those who need them. When was the last time you saw an advertisement for a "revolver only" course? Where do you go today to learn about the care and feeding of your pet revolver? This is in spite of the fact that the short-barreled wheel gun is very popular with the legally armed citizen and remains a favored backup gun for police. (For now, this probably applies mostly to those officers who transitioned from revolver to pistol. As their numbers dwindle, I suspect, so will police interest in the revolver for any purpose. (Just the other day I had a police instructor tell me he used to talk with his students about a gunfight he'd been in armed with an S&W Model 60. He said he got so many questions asking what kind of gun it was that he stopped telling the story.) Since the 4-inch revolver has been replaced by the pistol in police and military service, and since the big magnum revolvers are mostly used by hunters, it is possible that the mainstay revolver—the one most purchased, most carried, and most used—will become the snubby.

Consider this my effort, then, to ensure that the revolver, specifically the snub-nosed revolver, gets full credit for long, faithful, and continuing service (Part I: The Gun). With a little luck, it might also inspire some of those old-time revolver hands with considerably more knowledge than I have to share their experience and expertise. Consider also that this text will serve to highlight the tactical strengths that the little gun brings to those all-too-common personal-protection situations that blow up right in your face (Part II: The Tactics).

From 1975 until 1982, I was a police firearms and tactics instructor at the New Mexico Law Enforcement Academy. It was my job to teach police recruits in our basic classes and veteran officers in our advanced classes how to use lethal force to appropriately and effectively—how to survive the before, during, and after of an armed confrontation. The primary police-duty sidearm during this time was the double-action revolver. The S&W Model 19 4-inch backed up by the Model 36 Chiefs Special 2-inch was the most popular combination with the officers I trained. An NRA poll during those years showed that something like 97 percent of the police agencies in America issued the revolver.

As part of my duties, I was able to develop a program that allowed me to interview those police officers in our state who were involved in a shooting. Interestingly, not once during my conversations with more than 75 officers did anyone suggest that he or she would have been better served with a pistol. In fact, we had only one instance in which an officer had to reload. We had another incident in which the officer needed to reload but chose to run back to the patrol car and continue the affray with a double-barreled 20-gauge shotgun. All of the federal agencies carried revolvers and appeared to feel appropriately armed. During this time I was also privileged to be selected by the NRA's Police Instructor Program as an adjunct instructor. This experience allowed me to meet with officers from all across the United States and learn from them. Several of these officers belonged to agencies that had switched from the revolver to the pistol and back to the revolver.

The biggest problem we all shared was the ineffective terminal performance of the common duty rounds, the lead roundnose .38 Special and the semi-wadcutter lead .357 Magnum round. The FBI-designed 158-grain +P lead hollowpoint (LHP) solved the problem in both 4-inch and 2-inch .38 Special revolvers. By the time this round had gained national acceptance I had contacts within the firearms training units of most of the big city agencies that had adopted the LHP. Their reports were always the same: "Given good shot placement on the part of the officer, the LHP is a very reliable duty load in both our 2-inch and 4-inch service revolvers. One or two shots to the upper torso generally stops the actions of the bad guy."

So by the time I left the academy in 1982, we had a wide selection of revolvers from which to choose, an effective .38 Special load for the most popular police handgun, and the 125-grain jacketed hollowpoint in .357 Magnum, which promised to take care of the performance problems in that then-popular caliber as well. At this point I could say with considerable authority that with average shooting skill, sound tactics, and the survival mind-set, if the officer (armed with a revolver) did his part, he was likely to come through an armed encounter just fine. I had also learned that the little five-shot Chiefs Special was a sound concept as a bottom-line life insurance gun, especially in its role of backup. When you desperately needed "five for sure," this tough little revolver wouldn't let you down.

I left the academy to join CIA as what was then known as a paramilitary operations (PM) officer. To my great delight, I soon learned that one of the functions of a PM officer was to conduct firearms training for agency personnel. When I joined, agency-issue handguns were the Browning High Power (BHP) and the Smith & Wesson revolver in a variety of "K" and "J" frames. My firearms education continued.

Part of this education was the opportunity to pursue my avid interest in all things related to the Office of Strategic Services (OSS). I read everything I could get my hands on pertaining to OSS in the agency's extensive library. I had the opportunity to meet and talk with OSS vets. The confidence these men had in training that was about 40 years distant was incredible. As they talked, their hands still traced deadly patterns of long-ago-learned open-hand, knife, and handgun skills. They all remembered their chief instructor, William E. Fairbairn (as the Shanghai Buster), and my impression was that, among his many skills, he may have been the foremost combatives instructor of our time. He knew what to teach, how to teach it, and how to ensure that his students retained their skills and could produce them on demand in a tight situation. I also learned that the most frequently used skill among OSS operatives was the unarmed combat techniques they had been taught, with the handgun being a distant second. The firearm, usually the little Colt .32 ACP, was primarily used to prevent capture or facilitate an escape subsequent to being captured but before being incarcerated. Unfortunately, I was to learn that this is still a valid reason for an intelligence officer to be armed in a high-threat operational environment. This knowledge, coupled with my New Mexico experience, was to have a significant influence on the handguns I chose to carry when I had the option.

In early 1983 I spent several months in Beirut, Lebanon. While we were there my teammates and I were asked to provide firearms instruction for most of the agency officers in Beirut. During our stay we got to know them pretty well. Hence, the range training had a festive quality, and we wrapped it up with a superb Lebanese meal at a restaurant near the range. Several days later we flew back to headquarters (HQ). On 18 April, about 10 days after I had left Beirut, I stepped into an elevator at HQ and found myself sharing it with one of our secretaries. I knew by looking at her that something was very wrong. She had lost all of her color and appeared to be in shock. In a voice barely above a whisper she asked, "Have you heard? The Beirut Embassy has been bombed. They don't think any of our people survived."

William F. (Bill) Buckley, a senior paramilitary officer and one of my bosses at the agency's Counterterrorist Group, volunteered to go to Beirut as the new Chief of Station. Bill was frequently called back to HQ during this assignment, and on one such visit I bumped into him in the hallway and we talked shop for a few minutes. During the conversation, I noted that his hair had almost overnight gone gray. (NOTE: This year I had the opportunity to talk with Lieutenant Commander Mike Walsh, author of the book *SEAL!* Mike had served with Bill during Vietnam and was also in Beirut during this time. He made the same observation. Buckley was under enormous pressure.) On 16 March 1984, while watching CNN as I went through my morning exercise routine, I heard the announcer say that William F. Buckley, a Department of the Army civilian assigned to the Beirut Embassy, had been kidnapped. Buckley was tortured to death in captivity. One particularly haunting memory of this episode that remains with me is that of seeing Buckley's name still carried on the station's personnel roster as "COS-Missing" during subsequent trips to Beirut. His name was not removed from the roster until his body was returned to the United States in 1991. By all accounts, he was not armed when the kidnappers grabbed him as he walked from his apartment to his car to drive to work. To this day, I go over the events of Buckley's kidnapping in my mind, and I can't help but wonder how history would have been written had he been armed with a Chiefs Special stoked with LHPs.

Later, when I was an instructor at "the Farm" (the agency's training facility), I used Bill Buckley's story as one of about 25 case studies to remind our personnel of the realities of working overseas as an intelligence officer. At that time, all of our operations officers going to high-threat posts were trained in the use of the Browning High Power and the S&W Model 640. On their end-of-course critiques, they were likely to say that the BHP was a great gun, but they could see little use for the 640. "Hard to shoot" and "not enough bullets" were the most common complaints. Usually, we would travel twice a year to various stations to check on the training and to see if it was meeting the needs of the officers in the field. During these visits we would find nearly everyone had opted for the 640 when a gun was needed because it was easier to carry and conceal than the Browning was.

But I suppose the seed for this book was planted in the early 1990s during a visit to Quantico to discuss training issues with the DEA firearms staff. I had recently completed an overseas assignment that had required me to work closely with DEA agents responsible for conducting Operation Snowcap. I came away from the assignment with a much greater understanding of and appreciation for DEA's overseas counternarcotics enforcement efforts. Typically, once they found that I was being assigned to the agency's training facility, they offered me the full cooperation of their staff at Quantico.

It so happened that a Basic Agent class was in progress, and the instructors invited me to watch a raid exercise being conducted at their training "town." The students were a bright, fit mix of young men and women. (Actually, young is an understatement. They all looked to be about

15. But about then I'd noticed that everybody was starting to look younger than I did.) The "raid" took place with great enthusiasm, ending up in a major Simunitions shootout. Needless to say, the students had not done anything right, and the instructors pointed out their errors in excruciating detail. One of the major issues arose over an overlooked or ignored Model 65 S&W revolver that was lying on the floor beside some "dope." The instructors advised the students never to leave a firearm found during a raid unattended. The students were then ordered to set up outside the residence and told they would keep doing this until they got it right. This time they corrected all of the mistakes from their previous effort, and one young man policed up the revolver. Of course, there still ensued another substantial exchange of "FX" rounds as the raid team swept through the back rooms of the residence.

The instructors pretty much led the students to believe they would have to train for another year or two to get it right. Undaunted, the young student with the Model 65 proudly held it up and exclaimed, "Well, at least we didn't leave this lying around!" To which one of the instructors responded, "Good job. Now make it safe." Basic Agent Trainee Whoever looked at the revolver pretty much like a mule looks at a wristwatch. A small voice said, "Sir, I don't know how to get it open." Some guys tell me they know their age is starting to show the first time a young girl addresses them as "Sir." I gotta tell you, for me it was a young federal agent-in-training who didn't know how to open the cylinder on a handgun that had been the sidearm of choice for America's police only a decade earlier. Which, of course, was the point of the training. One of the instructors then gave an impromptu class on the revolver—much the same, I reminded myself, as we had conducted a similar class during the dark ages, only using a semiauto pistol.

This book assumes you have already determined whether the little revolver does or doesn't fit into your personal protection plan. (My one and only sales pitch will be to hope that you have also read *Defensive Living* (Loose Leaf Law, 2000). Dave Spaulding and I wrote that book, like this one, primarily for the private citizen. *The Snubby Revolver* is intended to complement *Defensive Living*.) You have my solemn oath that I will not try to sell you a snub-nosed revolver. (Actually, they're doing just fine without any help from me.) I also promise not to bore you with any sort of comparative debate over revolvers, pistols, ammo, and such. My only goal is that, after having read the following, you will be better equipped to maximize the tactical strengths of your snubby revolver, if that is your weapon of choice. I am going to pay particular attention to what I believe we now call extreme close quarters (ECQ), or from six feet (the reactionary gap) to contact, since this is prime street crime territory. It is also prime snubby territory.

You will also have a fuller appreciation of what others have done with the little gun, which has written, and continues to write, a rich history all its own. I am guided in my preparation of this book by some mighty good advice given to me years ago by an agent of the FBI: "Police don't need to be issued better weapons. They need to learn to better use what they are already issued." Certainly words to live by, and not just for police.

PART

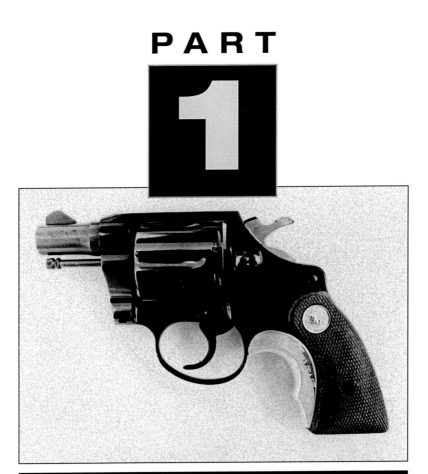

1

THE GUN

Why the Snubby?

BY WAY OF GETTING STARTED with this subject, let's take a little stroll down memory lane. We'll begin in 1930 with a book entitled *Shooting*, by J. Henry Fitzgerald, an employee of Colt for many years, and the designer of the "Fitz Special," a customized short-barreled Colt .45 New Service revolver:

> Some of the advantages of the 2-inch barrel are: in a scuffle the barrel is so short that the man holding the revolver has far more leverage than the man who is trying to take it away from him. As an arm to carry in an automobile the barrel is so short that the revolver may be swung either right or left across the steering wheel without striking it. . . . Sometimes even with new ammunition a defective shell is encountered and then

the two-inch barrel will help. I have never had a bullet stop in a 2-inch-barrel revolver. It is an undisputed fact that the short barrel is faster on the draw than the long barrel.

Next we have Fairbairn's classic *Shooting to Live*, published in 1942. He thought quite highly of the Fitz Special:

> Let us consider first the case of the detective or plain-clothes man. Here the weapon must be carried concealed and the wearer must be prepared for the quickest of quick draws and an instantaneous first shot, most probably at very close quarters. For that purpose, our own choice would be a cut-down revolver of heavy caliber [which he goes on to describe and credit Fitzgerald with].

Following World War II, one of the best books available on the snubby was *The Handgunner's Guide, Including the Art of Quick Draw and Combat Shooting* by Chic Gaylord, the famous holster maker:

> Handguns for concealment can be divided into two categories, the "carry gun" used by off-duty police officers, detectives and plain-clothes men; and the "hideout" used by undercover men or, as a secondary emergency weapon, by police officers desiring the insurance of a second gun. No carry gun should be of less than .38 caliber. A .38 Special is even more desirable. . . . One of the most effective carry guns that I have ever seen is the Webley & Scott .455 caliber Irish Constabulary model. This British handgun is not much larger than a Colt's Detective Special, yet it packs a wallop like Ingo Johannson's.

Early snubby examples: The Colt Agent and the S&W Model 12.
Both of these are easy-to-carry air-weight revolvers.

In Col. Rex Applegate's classic *Kill or Get Killed*, he applauds the introduction of the S&W Chiefs Special and the Centennial. It wasn't until a good many years later that we were to learn of his role in the development of the Centennial, based on an incident he was involved in using the .38 S&W cartridge in an S&W Safety Hammerless, the forerunner of the Centennial. As I understand it, Applegate was working in Mexico following World War II. He and a companion were attacked by a *campesino* wielding a machete. Allegedly, Applegate fired all five rounds of .38 S&W into their attacker with no effect. His companion terminated the incident with his .45 Colt 1911. Applegate talked S&W into bringing out the Centennial chambered for the .38 Special. His thinking was clearly guided by how he saw the small revolver:

> Any revolver so small that it can be covered by an ordinary man's hand, weighing 21 ounces or less and shooting the .38 Special cartridge, can hardly be considered as the ideal target weapon. Even though creditable scores can be achieved by using their fixed iron sights against conventional targets, such guns are designed, manufactured and intended for use against targets *that can shoot back*.

Bill Jordan, the famed Border Patrol officer, is considered by many as the dean of American combat revolver shooters. His law enforcement experience, combined with his U.S. Marine Corps wartime service, gave him a depth and breadth of gunfighting knowledge that few of us can ever hope to match. In addition to having Olympic-class hand-to-eye coordination, by all accounts, Jordan was also warmly regarded as a true Southern gentleman. His book, *No Second Place Winner*, is a treasure trove of useful information that may be beyond the skill level of most of us mere mortals. In it, he tells us what he sees as the role of the snubby:

These small, light guns (the airweight S&W Chief Special and the Colt Agent) have a definite value in plainclothes work. . . . When I am on duty and wearing a coat, I prefer to carry my regular service .357 Magnum. Off duty, or when the weather is hot, there is great temptation to conclude that there won't be any trouble anyway and go unarmed rather than either wear a coat or look conspicuous wearing a big gun without the coat to conceal it. That's the time when the little airweight model, slipped into a trouser pocket, is worth its weight in gold. And for such use, the smallest and lightest gun available, provided it has reasonable power, is best.

Some things endure because they do what they do better than anything that can be designed to replace them. And so it is with the short-barreled revolver. This little gun is so imminently suited to do what it does that its function has often doubled as its name, as in pocket pistol, hideout, backup, off-duty. These names also describe the tactical niche that this type of revolver fills. Today, at a time when the semiauto pistol has become the issue handgun for our police and military and the handgun of choice for a lot of our citizens, the snubby holds its own. It is available in a wider range of calibers, weights, and finishes than at any time in its history. It continues to serve as a dependable backup weapon for the police officer, and it is a highly popular choice with the legally armed private citizen.

Nowadays, the most popular snubby is probably the five-shot version, so I will pay a little extra attention to it throughout the book. But to be fair, by definition we will include in this category any five- or six-shot double-action revolver of caliber .38 Special or greater, with a barrel no longer than 2 1/2 inches and weighing 30 ounces or less. This allows us to include S&W's Model 19 2 1/2-inch .357 in the snubby category, as was the case in some of the old

Practical Pistol Course (PPC) matches. With its adjustable sights, this has to be considered a real Cadillac snubby. But more to the point of this book, we should not quickly forget that for a good many years this revolver was the standard-issue sidearm of the U.S. Secret Service. This was the gun that protected the president.

SNUBBY SUMMIT

As most of you probably know by now, Andy Stanford, of Options for Personal Security, hosted a program just for snub revolver users on December 3–5, 2005, at the Police Hall of Fame in Titusville, Florida.

The Snubby Summit was made special not only by the guest speakers and instructors Stanford invited, but also by the students. They were a serious group who came to learn. Accordingly, they were attentive, asked good questions, applied themselves fully, and paid close attention to the safety of themselves and others during the range exercises. They were the stars of the show.

Massad Ayoob was the keynote speaker and also gave a class on Shooting Through Clothing. Michael DeBethencourt gave a class on Snubnose Revolver Skills. Jim Cirillo discussed Snubby Ammo. Claude Werner conducted a course on Snubby Skills Development. Stanford did a class on Snubby as a Second Gun. Craig Douglas did his very popular presentation on Extreme Close Quarters (how to avoid and manage a confrontation). Jim Clark discussed Snubby Courses of Fire. Clyde Caceres did a presentation on Shooting from Awkward Positions. Tom Givens discussed Pocket Rockets, and I gave a presentation on Living With Terrorism.

Everybody agreed that Stanford has a winner here. He plans to make the snubby program a regular feature. If you're interested in attending an event that is both fun and a great learning experience for the dedicated snub gunner, get in touch with Stanford at OPS.

Andy Stanford
Options for Personal Security
P.O. Box 489
Sebring, FL 33871-0489
www.optionsforpersonalsecurity.com

The Gunfight and the Snubby

FIREARMS TRAINING PHILOSOPHY (courtesy of California Highway Patrol Officer Lou Chiodo):

The purpose of firearms training is to prepare an officer to use firearms in a fight against an adversary in what usually begins as a spontaneous attack initiated by the suspect. Our firearms program is not about shooting. It is about fighting. When the concept of fighting is taken out of firearms training, we have forgotten the purpose of our training.

I can clearly remember the first time I ever held a handgun that had been used *in extremis*. I was about 14, and we were visiting some friends. My dad and our host, both career Marines, were discussing their Korean War experiences, something my Dad never did with me. A mule team couldn't have pried me off the couch. Somehow the conversation turned to handguns, and in short order a Chiefs Special was produced. I now know it had to have been one of the early production models, complete with the diamond-style checkering, flat thumb piece, and all. According to my dad's friend, his unit was responsible for deactivating booby traps left behind in villages the Marines entered. A rifle got in the way due to the nature of the work, so everyone in the unit carried a handgun, most often the issue Colt .45 ACP 1911. However, getting the old warhorse into action with the flap holster and cold hands was a problem, which the Chiefs Special resolved. As I remember the story, upon entering a factory building of some type to check for booby traps one day, our host surprised one of the saboteurs in the act, and the little .38 Special rose to the task quite nicely.

It is interesting to note that while gunfighting equipment and training have evolved considerably over the years, the gunfight that is resolved by a handgun today looks no different than its historical predecessors. In its most common form, you will face a single assailant, and you will be alone as well. Your assailant will probably be armed with a handgun but may possibly be armed with a knife or blunt instrument. The distances will usually be less than 10 feet. It will be over very quickly. Reloading is rarely an issue. The confrontation may resemble nothing you have ever done in training.

• • •

The uniformed patrol officer, one of the department's few females, observed suspicious activity in the parking lot of a fast food restaurant. She parked the cruiser, got out, and approached two male subjects. A fight ensued, and the officer found herself down on all fours with one of the subjects straddling her back as he attempted to choke her to death with her nightstick. She drew her service revolver, a Model 15 .38 Special, brought it up in a motion similar to saluting, and thrusted it back over her right shoulder. The gun was

THE GUNFIGHT AND THE SNUBBY

now upside down, and the muzzle was pressed against her assailant. She pulled the trigger twice, killing him.

• • •

If your gun doesn't work or stops working, you may not have time to correct the problem.

• • •

Two plainclothes officers attempting to arrest a subject ended up fighting with the individual and were forced to shoot him. One officer was armed with a Browning High Power, which failed to fire. The second officer was carrying a two-inch Colt Lawman .357 Magnum. Fortunately, his gun worked just fine. Subsequent investigation revealed that during the struggle the BHP magazine popped out just far enough to activate the magazine safety. The culprit turned out to be poor holster design. A Tap-Rack-Bang would have gotten the BHP into action, but time had run out. The second officer saved the day.

• • •

All of which brings us to the three rules of gunfighting.

1) *Always have a gun.* The snubby is reliable, small, light, and powerful enough to ensure that we have no excuses for ever violating rule number one.

• • •

A community relations officer, he was one of the most popular officers in the department and well known throughout the city. He had just completed a crime prevention seminar at a civic group luncheon. He walked out of the building and into the armed robbery of a shoe store. The bad guy ran out of the store and jumped into a waiting car. The officer pursued the suspect and managed to get him to pull over. He approached the car and was gunned down.

Subsequent investigation revealed that the officer was not armed. (I wonder how this would have ended if he'd had a Colt Agent stuffed with LHPs ?)

• • •

2) Always gain and maintain the tactical advantage (cheat).

• • •

A detective who had just parked his car was locking the door when he was confronted by an armed robber who asked him to hand over his wallet. The robber was standing to the left rear of the officer, who was carrying a Chiefs Special in a shoulder holster. The officer cleared the handgun from the holster and fired through the back of his suit coat, killing the robber.

• • •

3) Never give up.

• • •

He was an aggressive state trooper with his department's record for number of stops and number of citations. On this particular day he had stopped three cars at once. As he sat in the patrol car writing the tickets, one of the drivers walked back to him armed with a handgun. He ordered the officer to remove his duty sidearm from the holster and to dump the ammo on the floor of the car. He then ordered the trooper out of the car and made him undress. In an inside pocket of his jacket the officer had a Chiefs Special loaded with the new Remington 95-grain JHP. As he dropped his coat to the ground, he drew the little gun and fired, killing his assailant.

• • •

In the next chapter we'll take a look at the requirements for the gun to be used in extremely close quarters, and you'll see why the snubby is a natural.

Requirements for the ECQ Handgun

BEFORE I DISCUSS the requirements for a handgun to be used in extremely close quarters, or why I chose the snubby, further explanation is in order. Specifically, during my agency service, unlike the police officer, I had the options of confrontation avoidance and strategic withdrawal (running away) available to me. Mainly this was because, contrary to the image of the international secret agent as depicted by Hollywood, the intelligence officer is often unarmed. For a variety of reasons, he may not have a handgun available to him. (If you think going into an "iffy" situation when armed makes you nervous, try it without being able to take comfort in the fact that at least you have a fighting chance!) So for those times when I was approved to carry a sidearm, I stuck with revolver simplicity over the Browning. Unlike the police officer, who becomes familiar with his sidearm through constantly carrying it and using

"Intelligence ... is the knowledge [usually obtained secretly] which our highly placed civilians and military men must have to safeguard the national welfare." —CIA senior analyst Sherman Kent.

it in high-stress situations, the intelligence officer is seldom able to "bond" with a handgun. (I know, I know, but bad puns are a habit I picked up from Charlie Phillips.)

Another tool I relied upon heavily was tradecraft, or the ability to conduct an intelligence operation or operational act without being detected. My whole lifestyle was low profile. My work required me to be constantly aware of what was going on around me. As one of my Special Air Service (SAS) friends likes to say, "We had to be invisible, not invincible." This is an especially important distinction to make because, in theory, if you practice good tradecraft as well as good personal security, you should be able to avoid any unpleasantness. Hence (according to the standard doctrine), a handgun is unnecessary. And in practice the concept actually works quite well. Most of the time. Unfortunately, nothing is Murphy-proof. You can do everything by the book and still get jammed up.

• • •

There was yet another crisis brewing, and Washington was screaming for more information. All leads, however small, were being followed up. This set of circumstances found a CIA operations officer and two military debriefers sitting in a hotel room waiting for an individual who claimed to have information on a terrorist attack that was about to take place. When it became obvious to them that the caller was a "no-show," they left the room. The two debriefers walked out of the room first, followed by the agency officer. As the case officer was pulling the door to the room closed, the trio came under fire from two men at a distance of about eight feet. The agency officer shoved the debriefers ahead of him as they ran away from the gunmen and toward the door to the hotel stairs. By the time they reached the stairs, the agency officer had been wounded. Their attackers, following closely behind the trio, tossed a hand grenade down at them as they raced down the steps. The only good news in the deal was that the grenade was of inferior quality, and no one was injured when it exploded. In the ensuing confusion, both parties got away. (Yep, you guessed it—I wonder what the outcome would have been if he'd had a Centennial stoked with LHPs stashed in a coat pocket).

• • •

1) *So my first requirement for the ECQ handgun is that it must be reliable.* We're talking reliable not only in terms of function but also in terms of reducing the chance for operator error, in terms of reducing the number of things that can go wrong. In a word, simplicity. In a word, operator-proof.

• • •

The undercover narcotics officer sat across the table from the subject of a "buy-bust" operation. As the situation began to fall apart, the officer drew his handgun, a stock 1911 .45 ACP. He pointed the pistol at the bad guy, who was now standing up firing, but the officer's pistol failed to fire and he was slain. According to witnesses, the top of the slide struck the edge of the table as the officer was drawing the pistol. Whether this caused the officer to inadvertently push the safety back on or whether it caused his thumb to miss the safety completely could not be determined.

• • •

2) *Since a holster may not be available or desirable, the handgun must be reliable if stored in nonholsters such as pockets, purses, and so forth.* (I've known police officers, acting as backup for another officer, to hide a snubby in a popcorn box, paper bag, lunch bucket, and such, when they needed to blend but be able to respond quickly.) Safeties don't change position, magazines don't fall out, pocket lint doesn't gum up the works, and so on.

3) *The handgun must be reliable when fired from unusual positions, through coat pockets, and the like.*

4) *The handgun must be reliable if the muzzle is jammed against your assailant.*

5) *The handgun must be reliable if you can't get the proper grip or lock your firing wrist.* This is a concern if you are forced to draw and fire while seated in a vehicle or during a struggle with your assailant.

I know of three cases in which officers were forced to shoot someone who had grabbed them from behind. (One of those incidents is described in an earlier chapter.) In two cases, the officers with revolvers (one used a 4-inch S&W, and the other had a Colt Detective Special) solved the problem. In the third instance, the officer was using a Colt 1911 and his hand position kept forcing his grip open to the point where he could not depress the grip safety and fire the gun. He finally solved his problem too, but it took some doing.

• • •

A number of years ago, the New York City Police Department (NYPD) did a study of a 10-year period during which officers of the department were involved in 6,000 armed confrontations. They could not document a single instance in which an officer's revolver failed to fire during one of these confrontations. Given the endless variety of things that can go wrong in a gunfight, I take great comfort in such information

• • •

He was an officer in the U.S. military, assigned as an advisor to the host government's military. The country in which he was stationed was combating a highly aggressive terrorist group that had killed 12 American servicemen in the last 18 months. Unbeknownst to him, he was next on their list. Two men followed him home on the day of the hit and rode up in the elevator with him. At the door to his apartment, they made their move. He sensed or heard them and turned. As he did so the shot intended for the back of his head struck him in the side of the face. He instantly attacked the two would-be assassins with the only weapon he had . . . his briefcase. They fled. (I wonder how this story would have ended had he been armed with a Ruger SP 101 stuffed with 110-grain SJHP .357 rounds.)

• • •

6) *If you are forced to grapple with your assailant, the weapon must have strong retention capabilities and still be able to fire.* To me this is the toughest gun fighting test—"kicking and gouging in the mud and the blood and the beer," but able to come up shooting.

• • •

. . . He began shooting at me, hitting me once in the back, the gas pumps a few times, and then me one last time in the chest as I turned to shoot him. However, my Beretta would not fire; the struggle had deactivated the trigger by releasing the magazine.

(From the February 1994 issue of *Combat Handguns* describing a shooting at a filling station.)

• • •

7) *After-market grips, especially rubber ones, should not stick to clothing or otherwise interfere with concealment.*
8) *The gun should have no sharp edges that could get caught in clothing.*

9) *If your choice is a revolver, the grips should not interfere with speedloaders.*

10) *The handgun should have a rust-resistant finish.*

11) *Elmer Keith's idea of the perfect carry handgun was the largest caliber you could shoot well. I would add that it should also be of a size, weight, and concealability that will encourage you to always have it with you, on your person.*

12) *The ECQ handgun should be capable of firing a bullet that has a documented gunfighting history of performance that meets or exceeds that of .45 ACP hardball.*

Colt .357 Magnum Carry with an Ashley Big Dot front sight.

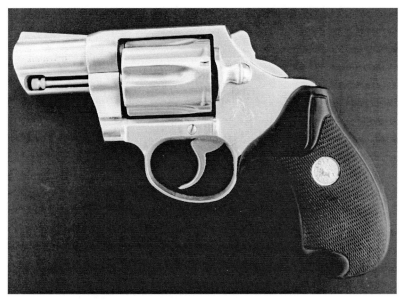

Colt Detective Special with factory night sight.

S&W 640 in .357 Magnum.

This officer's revolver was taken out of action by an assailant's bullet, which struck the front of the cylinder and lodged in the charge hole. A good reason to carry two handguns.

13) *Unless there are considerations that force you to choose otherwise, stick with the all-steel versions.* The all-steel five-shot revolvers, such as the J frame Chiefs Special, weigh about 20 ounces. With practice, you can learn to control +P .38 Special ammo in these little guns. Below this weight level, recoil becomes unpleasant and makes practice a grim event. Suggestion: give serious consideration to the six-shot snubby, especially if you are only going to carry one gun. The D frame Colt Detective Special weighs about the same as the Chief, while giving you a little more gun to hang onto, hence enhanced recoil control. The extra shot is a bonus!

These requirements apply equally to the handgun you choose as a backup to your primary sidearm if you carry two guns. As the name implies, a backup gun becomes the cavalry if your primary sidearm is taken away, out of action, empty, or inaccessible. I have a photo of a revolver that took a direct hit in the front of the cylinder during a traffic stop that erupted into a gunfight. The bullet went straight into one of the charge holes, effectively locking the cylinder. The officer, standing at the driver's window when his gun was hit, was not carrying a second weapon. He was saved by his partner. It is generally agreed that if you need a handgun, you tend to need it in a hurry. So, by extension, when you need a backup, chances are you need it in a real big hurry. Or you may have to arm another officer, or a friend, or a family member. The simplicity of the revolver really proves its worth here. Why complicate your life if you don't have to?

• • •

The off-duty officer was en route to the garage to have his take-home vehicle serviced. His shift lieutenant called for assistance on the radio. The officer met him and learned that he needed backup to handle an armed robbery in progress. When the officer informed the lieutenant that he was unarmed, the lieutenant handed him a five-shot Charter Arms .38 Special. The officer was about to get into a gunfight with a handgun he'd never fired before. As luck would have it, he was able to apprehend one of the subjects after a short foot pursuit. He put the person on the ground and then realized he had no handcuffs. As he knelt beside his prisoner, he heard footsteps. Before he could turn around, he heard the sound of a handgun being cocked. He spun quickly and fired at his assailant from a distance of about two feet, killing him. This one made the TV show *Top Cops* as the Danny Hawkes story. I was pretty happy with the outcome as well, since Danny had been one of my students at the academy.

Holsters

BECAUSE OF ITS SIZE, the snubby conceals well in some holsters but is very tough to hide in others, especially when worn on the belt. And because holster preference is a personal issue, you're simply going to have to experiment. Every holster choice we are discussing here is a compromise of retention, concealment, speed, and comfort. The following, then, should not be taken as solutions to your requirements as much as they are to mine. The best I can hope for is to maybe save you a little money.

An absolute requirement for me is to be able to put my hand on the gun I'm wearing under a coat, with seatbelt, and so on, while seated. I'm also averse to leaving a handgun in my car, so I don't rely on a separate handgun as a "car gun," nor do I rely on "car holsters." Everything must be on my person, close at hand, and when I leave it comes with me. The following three holster styles let me access

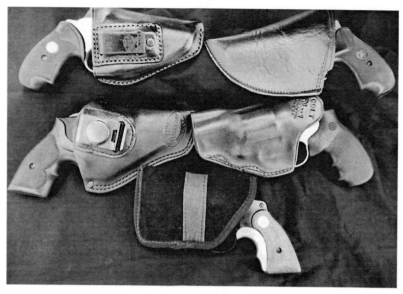

Clockwise from upper right: Mika pocket holster, Alessi Talon (Inside-the-waistband) new style, Uncle Mike's pocket holster, Bell Charter Oak IWB holster, Alessi Talon (old style).

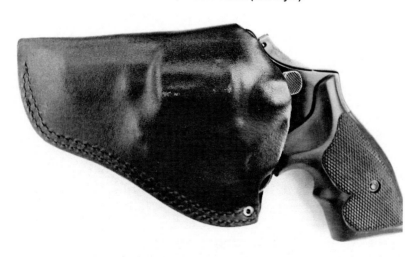

Close-up of Bell Charter Oak IWB holster.

the snubby with either hand, while seated, in close quarters, even on the john:

Inside-the-waistband crossdraw: This is my favorite carry method. I prefer the Alessi Talon, closely followed by the same model produced by Bell Charter Oak. This is worn under a loose-fitting garment, shirttail out. The popular Latin *guayaberras*, tee shirts, pullover sweaters, and the like all work well. The gun doesn't "print" when you reach or bend, a problem you experience with the hip holster.

Horizontal draw shoulder holster: Also by Alessi, for those coat-and-tie days because the crossdraw is hard for me to conceal under a jacket.

Ankle: This is my preferred carry option for a backup revolver. For me, the Renegade is the most comfortable of the breed. This allows me to keep two guns close at hand while seated.

While these three holsters meet the majority of my requirements, once in a while I need some alternatives. As I picked these alternatives over time, I tried to keep everything on the same side of my body and as close as possible to the same place as the above, while not giving up my seated requirement. As you will see, I wasn't always successful. Such is life.

Belly band: For a higher level of concealment and a corresponding tradeoff in quick access, I have frequently relied on an old Bianchi belly band (no longer available). Later versions that work well are offered by Uncle Mike's and Gun Video.

Pocket: Although it doesn't meet my seated requirement, it is certainly otherwise very handy for the lightweight backup revolver. I like the Uncle Mike's version best, followed by the Mika.

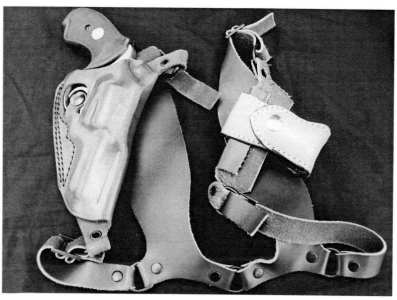

Early Alessi horizontal shoulder holster to which I added a speedloader pouch.

Renegade ankle holster.

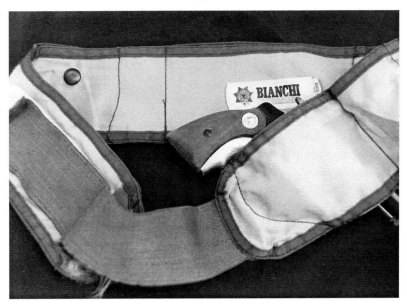

Early Bianchi belly band.

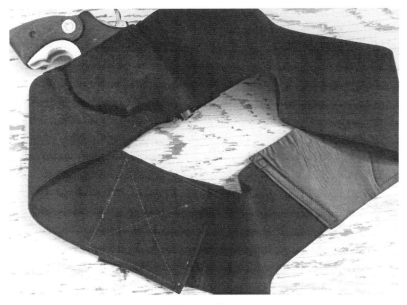

Gun Video belly band.

Bianchi fanny pack.

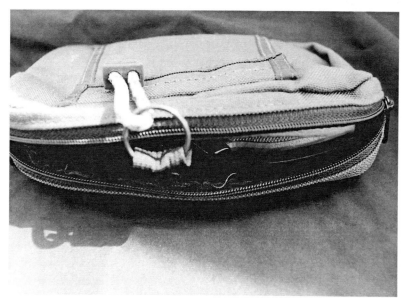

Uncle Mike's belt pack.

The Confidant: The holster in the tee shirt. Well-known holster designer Greg Kramer markets this nifty idea. It is especially useful for the traveler who wants to loss-proof his passport, traveler's checks, and such.

Barami Hip Grip: A handy option when you can't wear a holster and works very well in the car.

Belt pack: I've used the Gun Pak by Uncle Mike's and much prefer it to any of the fanny-pack concealable-carry methods. The fanny pack can be cut off of you and gone before you know it. We never lost a gun, but several cameras and wallets made somebody's day. The Gun Pak lets you carry your spare ammo easily and gives you an excuse to reach for your gun during a situation, as in, "Hand over your wallet !" OK, fine . . .

For the ladies . . . in my humble experience, the male who can tell the female of the species what type of holster to wear does not exist. It is definitely a female thing. For example, my favorite holster is the IWB crossdraw. I thought this might have possibilities for our female officers. When I asked them to try it out, to a woman, guess where they positioned it? Over their appendix. They could get away with it in some clothing styles, but it didn't give them much versatility. Next we tried the purse, which makes me especially nervous. They just seem to be trouble magnets. In my police days we had an officer lose her gun from her purse, in a vehicle during a prisoner transport. And, oh yeah—a shot was fired but no one got hit. In another instance, a narcotics officer ran out of ammo in a gunfight and his nearest reload was in his shoulder bag in the car. The shoulder strap is easily cut, the . . . well, you get the picture. As it turned out, my fears were groundless. The ladies didn't like them either. Not for any tactical reasons, mind you, but because they didn't go with their outfits! The closest we ever came to sort of a grudging acceptance were the Alessi horizontal shoulder holster and the Galco thigh holster.

Alessi Holsters, Inc.
2465 Niagara Falls Blvd.
Amherst, NY 14228-3527

Barami Corporation
6689 Orchard Lake Road #148
West Bloomfield, MI 48322

Bell Charter Oak Company
P.O. Box 198
Gilbertsville, NY 13776

Galco International, Ltd.
2019 W. Quail Ave.
Phoenix, AZ 85027

Gun Video
4585 Murphy Canyon Road
San Diego, CA 92123

Kramer Handgun Leather
P.O. Box 112154
Tacoma, WA 98411

Mika's Pocket Holsters
Rt. 1, Box 1234
Readstown, WI 54652

Renegade Holster and Leather Company
P.O. Box 31546
Phoenix, AZ 85046

Uncle Mike's
P.O. Box 13010
Portland, OR 97213

Grip, Front Sight, Trigger

THE GRIP, FRONT SIGHT, AND TRIGGER are three of the four most common complaints about the snubby (the fourth being ammo capacity—see Chapter 6). In this chapter we'll take a look at what we can do to remedy these issues.

GRIPS

One big advantage of the revolver is that you can change the grips on the handgun to better suit your hand. The grip can be made bigger or smaller, longer or shorter, skinnier or fatter, harder or softer. The real importance of this is that you will always do your very best work with a gun that fits your hand. A good fit helps the gun point better and allows you to control recoil better, which means you can shoot faster. These factors become especially critical if you are forced to shoot with only one hand.

By simply changing grips, the revolver can be made to fit almost any hand size.

Almost all of today's snubbies come standard with some sort of synthetic grip. That's the good news. In addition to helping dampen recoil, they keep the gun from twisting in your hand. This aids in rapid-fire control of the weapon as well as handgun retention. For all the above reasons, if I have wooden stocks on a revolver, I prefer them checkered, not smooth. They are a little tougher on your hand during a range session, but that's a small price to pay.

The single biggest complaint I have against most grips available today is that many of them still interfere with the smooth operation of the speedloader. (The mastery of the speedloader is a critical skill for the revolver shooter. I'll go into more detail on this in the next chapter.) It is usually not possible to check this out until you bring the gun home. Be prepared to replace the grips if you can't experiment on someone else's gun before you buy.

Another thing to consider in grip fit is how much concealment you really need. Many of the grips designed to help you conceal the small revolver do not leave any room for your little finger. In my case, other than for ankle carry, I have found that proper holster selection will allow me to conceal the extra grip length required to give my pinky finger purchase. Being able to use your whole hand to grab and grip the snubby will be a big aid in your ability to shoot it quickly and accurately.

How do you know if you have a grip that fits your hand? Try the following:

- The simplest test is to determine whether your grip allows you to control the double-action trigger. So, with an empty gun in hand, assume a proper firing grip. You should then be able to wrap your trigger finger around the trigger easily, almost up to the first joint (in my case), without having to adjust your grip on the revolver. This grip must allow your finger to pull the trigger easily while keeping the gun on target.

- Now try dry-firing the gun. If you are at home, remember—no distractions, empty handgun, EMPTY handgun, EMPTY HANDGUN!!! Come to the ready position, pick the target you want to hit, close your eyes and quickly bring the gun up to the target, open your eyes and check the front sight. Is it on target, up, down, left, etc.? Once this starts to feel right, do the same thing but pull the trigger twice before opening your eyes.

- Now start with the weapon holstered. Pick the target you want to hit. Draw the weapon, closing your eyes when your hand wraps around the grip. Open your eyes and check your front sight. Draw as quickly as you can. Try one hand first, then two hands. Every time you open your eyes you should see your front sight on the spot you picked to hit.

- On the range, from the ready and from the holster, shooting at an 8 1/2 x 11 sheet of typing paper as quickly as you are able, you should be able to keep all of your shots on the paper out to 21 feet. If you have to readjust your grip after drawing the weapon, you may need to change the grip. (Before changing anything, have someone who knows what to look for watch your drawing procedure. You need to be able to obtain the correct firing grip from the holster. Once your hand grips the revolver and withdraws it from the holster, nothing should move or change position.) If you have to readjust your grip after firing the revolver, you may need to change the grip. Shoot using one hand and then both hands. If you shoot using both hands exclusively, you may mask the problem. These simple tests will quickly reveal grip defects.

FRONT SIGHT

The front sights on today's snubbies are bigger and easier to see than those on earlier models but there is still a lot of room for improvement, especially when you compare them to the sights available on the popular small-frame semiautos. Some will even suggest that given the role of the short-barreled revolver, it really doesn't need sights at all. I disagree. This is the kind of thinking that can lead to an "adventure." An adventure is often caused by a lack of prior planning.

Let's review what we know today about the use of sights:

1. If the situation allows enough time, distance, and lighting, and good cover is available, we should obviously use the sights on the handgun and should have no trouble doing so. Under these conditions we are likely to feel that we are in control of the situation.

2. However, as we start to lose these elements, we also begin to lose our perception of being in control, and we now understand that we are (possibly) going to have to fight our assailant for tactical dominance of the situation. At this point, using the sights starts to become harder to do.

3. If we are attacked at close range and we didn't anticipate it and we suddenly fear for our life or the threat of serious bodily harm, the sympathetic nervous system may kick in. We are now subject to the effects of survival stress, which can cause us to have tunnel vision and to lose our near vision, among other things. No near vision = no front sight. The most recent documentation of this I can find today is in Lt. Col. Dave Grossman's latest book, *On Combat*.

4. The effects of aging cause the eyes to have trouble seeing that front sight. Presbyopia (aka Birthday Candle Disease) can set in anytime after we reach 40. Basically, the lens of our eye loses flexibility and quits focusing as it used to. Bifocals can correct the problem, which is great if you are reading a book; however, if you are trying to pick up a "flash" sight picture to quickly solve your problem, you may get at best a

blurry image and with stainless-on-stainless, you won't see anything at all.

5. And finally, when our life is in deadly danger we will instinctively keep our vision focused on the threat because we need that visual feedback to tell us how we should be reacting. (Are we hitting him? Did he drop the weapon?) Hence the term, "target focus." I recently read an account of a gunfight in which the officer stated that he started with his eye on the front sight but as the situation escalated he literally felt his vision being ripped off the front sight so he could watch his assailant.

So what can we do to enhance our visual capabilities, as well as the snubby's, to prepare us for a critical incident?

TRAINING

Good training is the best thing you can do for yourself to develop and hone your fighting skills. Training gives you the ability to use your equipment skillfully. If you are not skilled in the use of your handgun, hanging more aftermarket doodads off of it won't help. I saw this graphically when night sights first became popular—the shooters who were still struggling with the basics of grip-front sight-trigger got no benefit from the sights even though they were much easier to see in low light.

The really good news is that top-notch instruction in target-focused shooting is now available to military, law enforcement and the legally armed citizen who possesses a CCW permit. One of the foremost instructors in this skill, Lou Chiodo, has retired from police service and is now teaching fulltime. He can provide quality firearms instruction to you at all levels. His force-on-force training, using Air Soft guns and his protective gear, is one of the reasons his agency enjoyed a significant increase in hit rate in actual gunfights.

Chiodo has done and continues to do intensive research to make sure that this training meets his demanding standard. "Target-focus shooting is a technique designed to allow the user to respond quickly and with combat accuracy when confronted with a spontaneous unanticipated attack by an assailant in a variety of lighting conditions. Engagement ranges progressively work from contact distances to approximately 30 feet using target-focused shooting. Also, the use of the sight system is integrated into the curriculum to ensure that the full potential of the handgun can be exploited by the operator."

What you get when you train with Chiodo is, first and foremost, quality instruction in target-focus shooting technique taught at gunfight distances and times. You get a diagnostic testing and evaluation methodology that ensures that you have mastered all of the required skills, and you may proceed confidently to the next level of instruction. And you will undergo the practical application of your training in Air Soft force-on-force simulations that are based on today's street realities. To contact Lou Chiodo, visit his Web site at www.gunfightersltd.com.

XS BIG DOT TRITIUM

Next on the list of things you can do to improve the snubby's sights is the XS (formerly Ashley) Big Dot front sight. Dave Spaulding, another retired cop with in-depth knowledge of the combat handgun, believes that you really do yourself a favor and increase your chances of being able to pick up and use your front sight if you make it easy to see. He is a big believer in contrasting colors. He covers the subject in detail in his book, Handgun Combatives. The Big Dot offers both contrast and size to help you see it. In the accompanying photos (courtesy of XS Sights) you can see that at close range whether you focus on the front sight or focus on the target, the shooter's view of the Big Dot is virtually the same.

Whether you focus on the target ...

... or the front sight, you can still see that Big Dot.

Crimson Trace's Lasergrips have a new, compact "boot grip" style.

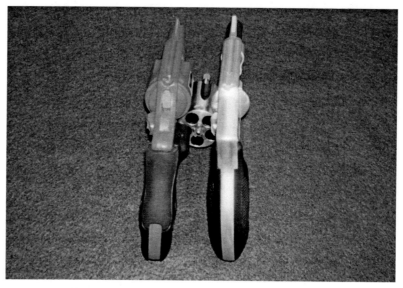

Boot-grip style Lasergrips shown from the rear.

Lasergrips still conceal easily.

The S&W 640 .357 "full up" with Lasergrips and the Big Dot sight.

CRIMSON TRACE LASERGRIPS

Since I'm not a big fan of widgets and gadgets, especially those that use batteries, I avoided the laser idea for years. But once I had the chance to spend some time with Clyde Caceres, the vice president of business development for Crimson Trace, I came up with some things about their Lasergrips that you need to know if you don't already; things that might help you decide if this is a piece of equipment that you can use.

First, and the most important, Lasergrips are steadily developing a serious reputation on the street. In fact, in the 17 documented gunfights involving officers using Lasergrips, the hit ratio is a little over 90 percent, very consistent with the significant increase in hit rate obtained by Lou Chiodo's target-focus-trained officers. Another important similarity in the case of both Chiodo and Lasergrips, all of their incidents involved uniformed officers, not the high-speed SWAT ninjas. This is an important point because the patrol officer is most likely to be faced by the type of gunfights Chiodo describes, which simply blow up in your face with little or no warning. As others have said, "It is pretty much a come-as-you-are affair. There are no engraved invitations to a gunfight." I am of the opinion that Lasergrips supplement target-focus training because you train like you fight.

Next, Caceres put me in touch with Rich Verdi, a recently retired police officer who is well known as a law enforcement firearms instructor. Verdi conducted a test with his agency that you should know about. He first had the officers fire their standard qualification course; those officers who wore glasses or contacts on a daily basis wore them and used the handgun sights. Then he had the officers fire the qualification course a second time; sights were still used, but officers had to remove their glasses or contacts.

Verdi noted that in this group, the officers who were not allowed to wear their corrective eyewear shot poorly. They were not as fast as they needed to be because they were losing time trying to get some sort of visual confirmation of the gun in relation to the target. Consequently, there was also a loss of confidence and, as we know, confidence is an essential fight-winning ingredient.

Verdi had the officers fire the course a third time; corrective eyewear was still out, but officers used Lasergrips. On this run, Verdi observed that the scores returned to the same level as those recorded on the first run—the officers were able to shoot quickly and their confidence was back. They now knew that even with uncorrected vision they could stay in the fight. Officers who didn't need visual aids learned that if they had blurry vision due to a dose of OC or possibly from a blow to the head, they could still do what they needed to do.

Another point that I think you need to consider is the intimidation factor of the laser. Both in the United States and in today's war zones, the intimidation factor of that little red dot is noteworthy. Crimson Trace has numerous anecdotal accounts from officers who have used Lasergrips in confrontations with hardened criminals who were ignoring the officers' commands, even though the officer was pointing a gun at the bad guy. However, as soon as they saw that red dot on their chest, they underwent an attitude adjustment and immediately began to comply.

Crimson Trace has about 40,000 Lasergrips in service with the U.S. military in Iraq and Afghanistan. They are finding that the laser apparently overcomes the language barrier and is credited with preventing needless loss of life. For instance, in situations where the soldiers are trying to get a car approaching a roadblock to stop, they don't speak the language and the car keeps coming even after warning shots have been fired. As a last ditch effort the laser is used and the car slams to a halt. They check the car out and may find it contains innocent civilians.

And finally, Lasergrips can save the day, once again, if you find yourself forced to fire from a position you do not practice on the range. You may be knocked down, injured, or simply unable to get the gun to eye level. Put the dot where you want the bullet to go and control the trigger.

At this point I still have a lot to learn about Lasergrips. And for sure you'll have to make up your own mind about whether they are for you or not. One thing I think I can say for certain though. If you ever try one on a snubby, don't be surprised if you find that some things are non-negotiable.

Lt. Col. Dave Grossman
P.O. Box 9280
Jonesboro, AR 72403
www.killology.com

Lou Chiodo
Gunfighters Ltd.
P.O. Box 212273
Chula Vista, CA 91921-2273
www.gunfightersltd.com

Dave Biggers
XS Sight Systems
2401 Ludelle Street
Ft. Worth, TX 76105
www.xssights.com

Looseleaf Law Publications
P.O. Box 650042
Fresh Meadows, N.Y. 11365-0042
www.looseleaflaw.com

Clyde Caceres or Jason DuVal
Crimson Trace Corporation
8089 SW Cirrus Drive
Beaverton, OR 97008
www.crimsontrace.com

TRIGGER

While the snubby can be purchased with both double- and single-action capability, I prefer the double-action-only version. The ability to cock the revolver and fire it single-action is an option that some favor in case they have to make a precision shot with the snubby. My concern stems from the problems arising from our training in the days when we used to teach both methods of firing the revolver. Invariably, during a critical incident, when the adrenaline was flowing and the fine motor skills were gone or going, an officer would cock the revolver and then cause it to fire when he didn't mean to. Or he would forget—again under stress—to decock the revolver and would put it back in the holster, still cocked. Once in a while he would discover, much to his dismay, that certain holster configurations or misplaced fingers would snag the trigger, now requiring about three pounds of pressure to fire, and . . . I know one highway patrolman who discharged his revolver in this fashion. He was involved in a felony stop and cocked his revolver in the process. The bad guys gave up without a fight, and the officer covered the two felons while his partner handcuffed them. The officer then reholstered his weapon to help his partner put the prisoners in the patrol car. As he inserted the revolver into his holster, still cocked, it discharged. The round traveled down the stripe on his uniform trousers before burying itself in the ground next to his ankle. (Which brings up the subject of decocking the revolver. Please see the photos on pp. 44–45, which illustrate the proper decocking sequence when the revolver is cocked and you decide not to fire.)

The double-action-only trigger does not make the gun safe. Even when many of the major departments issued double-action-only revolvers, there were still negligent discharges. The double-action trigger does provide the user with a little greater margin for error. I recall several cases in which officers told me they were able to stop the double-

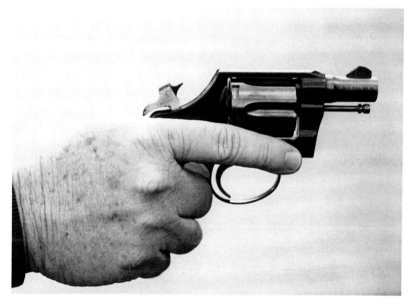

Cocked revolver.

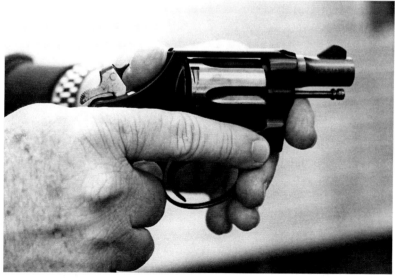

Place your weak-hand thumb between the hammer and the frame.

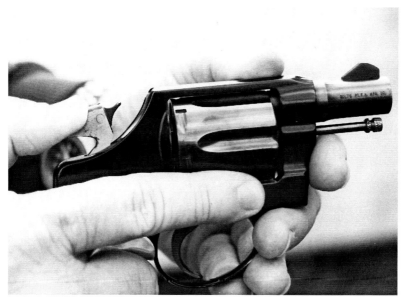

Pull the trigger, take your finger off the trigger, place strong-hand thumb on hammer spur, remove weak-hand thumb from under hammer.

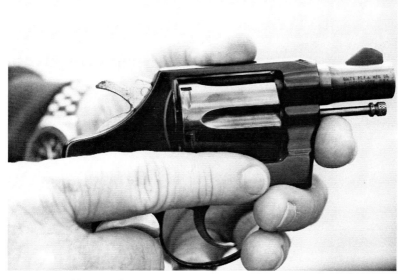

Hammer is now returned to double-action mode.

action firing stroke before firing the handgun when a suspect dropped the gun or knife or their partner stumbled into them. In other situations they were able to block the trigger during a struggle for the weapon by inserting a finger into the trigger guard behind the trigger. The double-action-only trigger system has become popular today with the pistols carried by many police agencies because it is more stress-proof than a single-action trigger. This is an especially important feature in a handgun that will frequently be pointed at people in high-stress situations.

The mastery of the double-action trigger requires the shooter to pull the trigger straight to the rear smoothly without stopping. Yanking the trigger and pulling or pushing it to one side or the other (instead of straight to the rear) can cause a miss even at close range. Good trigger control depends on the proper grip and fit.

Snubby Loads

DEFENSE LOADS FOR
THE 2-INCH BARREL

During the time I was an instructor at the academy we made several trips to Chihuahua, Mexico, to train the police there as part of the "sister state" agreement. Each U.S. border state had a Mexican sister state, and there were a number of different exchange programs. These trips were very educational for me, and the Mexican hospitality was absolutely first rate. In fact, on one trip they even invited my family down. My wife and daughters still talk about probably the closest thing to a vacation we enjoyed when the girls were little.

During one of these visits, I had just completed a class and we were getting ready to take a lunch break when one of the students walked up and handed me a Colt .45 1911 with very ornate silver grips. I thought he wanted me to look at his weapon, but it turned out he just wanted me to hold it for him as he unbuttoned his shirt and then pulled it up. Through the translator I learned that this officer had been in a number of confrontations. He pointed to one scar and said, ".38 Special [lead round nose], no problem." He pointed to a second scar and said the same thing. He pointed to a knife scar and said, "Knife, small problem." Then he showed me two scars on his right forearm that matched a corresponding scar on his abdomen. The translator said that the officer had been hit in the arm by a .45 slug, which had gone through his arm and into his stomach. The officer then pressed his arm to his stomach to show me the path of the bullet and said, ".45, big problem."

This was a defining moment for me. As a serious student of terminal wound ballistics, I had spent years studying charts and tables of muzzle velocities and foot-pounds of energy, ballistic gel photos, and so forth (most of which I didn't understand, truth be told). Yet here everything I really needed to know on the subject was summed up by a tough Mexican street cop with the scars to prove it. Assuming the shooter does his part and delivers the round(s) to the appropriate area on his assailant, is the bullet in question highly likely, likely, or highly unlikely to cause the recipient "big problems?"

While 230 grains of full-jacketed .45 ACP hardball may not be a death ray ("They don't always fall to hardball"), it certainly has a proven track record in a lot of close-quarter confrontations, including those of Alvin York, W.E. Fairbairn and the Shanghai police, the Texas Rangers, the U.S. Army's Special Operations Forces, and LAPD SWAT. It is a pretty good place to start as a stopping power standard for an ECQ handgun. It has caused a lot of bad guys "big problems."

We drew the line under .38 Special in our definition of what a snubby is because little guns provide little stopping power. I am also not very much into trends. I prefer to have a lot of documented field testing on the guns and loads that I select for personal protection. And such is the case with the 2-inch revolver and the lead hollow point (LHP) +P .38 Special. We now have about three-quarters of a century of experience with the Colt Detective Special, half a century with the Chiefs Special, and a quarter of a century with the LHP. Most all of the studies of actual street shootings (regardless of whose study it is) agree that the LHP (regardless of manufacturer) from a 2-inch revolver performs very much like .45 ACP hardball. It may not be a giant killer (depending on your definition of giant); however, according to an FBI agent I knew, the first man they shot with the LHP weighed about 300 pounds. He took one hit "plumb center," attempted to take a step, and fell flat on his face. Initially produced for the FBI by Winchester, it is now also available from Federal and Remington. This round was used by many of the major U.S. police agencies, the FBI, and a number of other federal agencies, plus the Royal Canadian Mounted Police. Actually, I think the Canadians used a slightly hotter version of the U.S. loading.

Once I get away from the LHP I have to plead ignorance. I have very little firsthand performance info on other bullet styles and weights. I do know that as revolver weight diminishes the LHP becomes less fun to shoot. More to the point, it becomes hard to control. Since bullet placement is the key to stopping power, ultimately you will be the judge of what you carry. If you can't shoot your load of choice quickly and accurately, keep practicing. If you still aren't satisfied you may get better results with a change in ammo. Usually (but not always), going to a lighter bullet will help. There are some really dandy new rounds available to us today in the 110- to 125-grain bullet weights that are probably going to become increasingly popular with those favoring the titanium revolvers.

If you are not comfortable with the .38 Special, the short-barreled revolver is also available in .357, .44 Special, .41 Magnum, and .45 Long Colt. As a great fan of the British

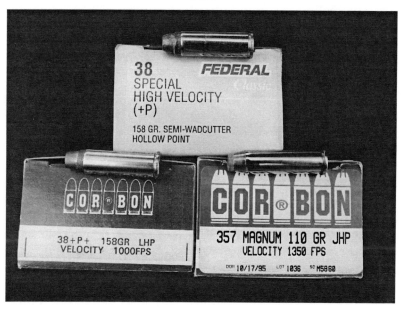

My preference is the +P or +P+ 158-grain lead hollowpoint in .38 Special and the 110-grain semijacketed hollowpoint in .357 Magnum.

bulldog concept, when Charter Arms produced its .44 Special Bulldog, I had to have one. This little gun was my close companion for several years, and just looking at those big 200-grain Winchester Silvertips gave me great peace of mind. The Charter Bulldog also established my preference for a concealed-carry gun weighing no more than 25 ounces.

Today, with the variety of "pocket rockets" we have available, if I feel I need to upgrade the horsepower available to me in a snubby, I go straight to the .357. I am very fond of the .357 (you have to be to shoot it in a snubby!). This is another round for which we have excellent street documentation. Although the 125-grain semijacketed hollowpoint (SJHP) is king in this load, I prefer the 110-grain semijacketed hollowpoint (SJHP) because it produces less recoil, especially in the snubby. On reflection, a pocket .357 Magnum may be an oxymoron. But it is a truly bad-to-the-bone streetfighter, especially when employed in the ECQ snubnose concept. Select the brand that produces the least muzzle flash or at least the dullest muzzle flash. Federal and Cor-Bon are probably the most popular choices in this load. There ain't much you can do about the ferocious muzzle blast, and yes, it kicks, but THIS is a bulldog . . .

EXOTIC AMMO

Much like I avoided the laser, I avoided exotic ammo for years. When asked why, I used my ever-faithful "too" defense. When I was first exposed to exotics in the mid-'70s they were too new (unknown, untested, hence unreliable). They were too expensive. There were too few incidents in which they were used for me to make any real evaluation of their capability. They were too special-purpose. (The air marshals were rumored to carry them, but no one I knew in those days had ever met a real air marshal, so there was some doubt as to whether they even existed or not.)

Everything I was able to find in print on the exotics of that time, which was precious little, said they either performed miracles or failed miserably. In fact, there was a story circulating (to this day I don't know if it was true or not) that a well-known exotic had been used by a hostage rescue force on an airplane assault. The rounds wouldn't penetrate the aircraft seat backs that the terrorists were using for cover; consequently, it took more time than it should have for the good guys to neutralize the bad guys.

No one that I knew used exotics, so I didn't pay much attention to them until the Strasbourg test was published. An exotic named MagSafe was the clear winner in virtually every caliber tested. I had hoped that these new findings would encourage agencies to give this round a try, but 10 years later I'm still waiting. More to the point, I made a couple of phone calls to folks I figured would have the latest info on their performance and they were no help at all.

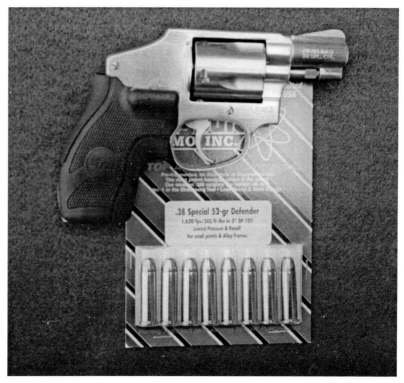

The MagSafe Defender load, made specifically for alloy-frame handguns.

In conversation with Joe Vega, the production manager at MagSafe, it appears that his customers, like his ammo, are highly specialized. He gets calls from time to time from shooters telling him that the ammo works as advertised. More to the point, he gets calls from time to time from medical examiners asking him how this round is intended to perform. I guess we should note the obvious here—the ME's office is also saying that it is clearly in possession of evidence to support the fact that MagSafe performs as advertised.

Just in case you missed the Strasbourg tests, they were a privately funded attempt "to isolate the physical mechanism responsible for rapid incapacitation of man-sized tar-

MagSafe's +P+Max .38 Special load.

gets and to disseminate these findings along with the test results to the military and federal law enforcement agencies." They did this using large, adult male French Alpine goats that were hooked up to various monitoring devices before being shot. All shots were aimed at the lung area of the animal and fired from a distance of 10 feet. The personnel involved in these tests concluded that "the most effective ammunition available for an unobstructed lung strike is the high-velocity type which uses pre-fragmented or fragmenting projectiles or those types that cause immediate expansion on impact." Ammunition used in the test included the various brands of commercially available con-

 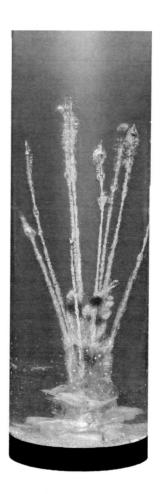

The gelatin block on the left shows 9 inches of penetration from a .38 Special Max +P round fired from a Ruger SP-101 with a 3-inch barrel. The one on the right shows 8 inches of penetration from a .38 Special SWAT round fired from a S&W Chiefs Special with a 2-inch barrel. Photos courtesy of MagSafe Ammo, Inc.

ventional SJHP/JHP rounds in pistol and revolver calibers from .380 ACP to .45 ACP. Two commercially available exotics were also included. As I noted earlier, MagSafe was the knockout champ in the testing.

What exactly is MagSafe? It is a round designed to give MAGnum performance with SAFEty. And it does all this with less recoil! What you see when you look at the round is a bullet jacket filled with shotgun pellets held in place with epoxy, but it is way more technical than that. You may have seen the advertisements for it in various publications. One look at that picture says it all. That spray of pellets upon impact is devastating.

There are several MagSafe variations available depending on caliber, but in the .38 I initially focused on the Defender. This is the company's bread-and-butter load for each caliber and the one designed (in .38 Special) for alloy-frame revolvers. I had the opportunity to look at some recent gelatin testing of this round and it performed as advertised. The 52-grain Defender load was fired from a 2-inch barreled .357 Taurus revolver at a distance of 5 feet. Muzzle velocity was measured at 1,346 fps. The gelatin block was covered by the following layers of clothing: a heavy winter coat, a flannel shirt, a T-shirt, and a long underwear pullover. The round went through the clothing, impacted the gelatin, and dispersed the pellets to a depth of 8 inches. I'll let you draw your own conclusions.

Back to the recoil issue, I shot this load in my Colt Agent, alongside Federal's 125-grain Nyclad hollowpoint, non +P, designed for use in snubbies, as a comparison. The Nyclad produces classic but controllable recoil. (The gun recoils against your hand sharply and you have to hang on to control muzzle flip.) The MagSafe Defender recoils against your hand more slowly and there is no muzzle flip. It is very controllable.

As a word of caution, we shouldn't forget that light rounds have a tendency to shoot low or below point of aim. With my Colt this began to occur at about 5 yards. For scenarios involving the armed citizen, home defense, and back-up gun requirements, 5 yards is a long way. An advantage to the light bullet weight is that spare ammo weighs next to nothing, so a speedloader full of ammo carries unnoticed.

I should add that I use the +PMAX .38 Special in my all steel snubbies. Vega has worked up these loads based on performance from a 2-inch Chiefs Special and they factor in the light bullet problem. (Note: According to Vega, MagSafe has done this with all the current .38 Special loads he offers.) They should be on (point of aim/point of impact) in your gun out to about 21 feet. However, since each gun is different you should test them in your handgun so you'll know for certain.

My sampling of MagSafe use in the field is way too small to draw big conclusions but their performance is certainly consistent with the Strasbourg findings.

Here is an example that I learned of from an officer who knew I was looking for information on shootings with MagSafe rounds: A man came home to find his girlfriend in bed with another guy. Caught in the act, the new boyfriend got out of the bed and attempted to talk his way out of the situation. The old boyfriend responded by shooting him at a distance of about 10 feet. He used a .380 pistol loaded with the .380 MagSafe Defender, a 60-grain projectile with a muzzle velocity of between 1,360–1,500 fps depending on the handgun used. The bullet passed through the luckless lover's sternum and clipped the top of his heart, shredding the arteries. The victim turned away from his attacker and dropped dead. At autopsy, his heart was found to be in two pieces.

Joe Vega
MagSafe Ammo, Inc.
4700 S. U.S. Hwy. 17-92
Casselberry, FL 32707

Speedloading the Snubby

WE NEED TO KEEP THIS IN PERSPECTIVE. Most gunfights are resolved within the capacity of the five or six rounds the revolver carries. Reloading is necessary in about 10 percent of the documented gunfights involving revolvers. There is also a great deal of truth to the fact that if you have to reload during the gunfight, you are either missing a lot or you brought the wrong weapon. Reloading after the shooting stops amounts to good tactics. So when you practice, spend most of your time on hitting. Get in the habit of reloading quickly, whether you need to or not, during range training (the reason being that if you need to reload, you'll probably have to do it pretty quickly), and your speed will develop naturally.

The fastest revolver reload is a second revolver, a.k.a. "the New York reload." I should think that the little featherweight titanium revolvers are going to be very popular in this role. I don't guess they weigh much more than a speedloader! If you shoot your primary gun empty, shove it in a pocket and get the lightweight backup into action. Two little guns equaling the weight of one big one should also do away with any excuse for not carrying something with you at all times.

• • •

Two big-city cops responded to a man-with-a-gun call. They encountered an individual armed with a handgun on the steps of an apartment building. The officers were using the vehicle for cover—one behind the trunk and one behind the engine compartment—when the shooting started. Both officers emptied a six-shot service revolver and a five-shot Chief before the subject went down. Out of the 22 shots they fired, they had hit him 18 times. One of the officers told me they never could have reloaded as fast as they were able to get the backup guns into action. They knew they were hitting their attacker, but he continued to fire as he came toward them. This was possibly one of the very first shootings involving an individual on PCP.

• • •

The second fastest way to load the revolver is with a speedloader. For the last quarter century or so, my preference has been Safariland. I've carried them in all sorts of climates, usually in a pocket, and they've never failed to function. Another reason I like them is because they do not require your hand to change position to activate the loader. Reloading the revolver has sufficient complexity without adding to it. Once you get your hand on the Safariland speedloader, you simply "dump and go."

When I went through the academy, we were required to reload revolvers from our pants pockets, although we would be carrying our spare ammo in loops or dump pouches. Fifty rounds of wadcutter, yessir. This experience gave me a whole new definition of slippery. Then we went through a period where speedloaders were specifically not allowed. They were OK for competition, but not for duty. Loops, dumps, and strips only were acceptable. Finally, the manufacturers got the bugs worked out and speedloaders were approved for duty use. Some of us never looked back. So step one is getting the (Safariland) loader loaded. A Los Angeles County Sheriff's Department range officer showed me this technique a good many years ago:

- Make sure the "star" is flush with the front of the loader.
- Insert the rounds.
- Using a "C" clamp grip, pinch. This depresses the speedloader spring.
- With your free hand, turn the body of the speedloader counterclockwise until you hear it click.
- Put the speedloader wherever you normally carry it. Revolver ammo is usually carried on the strong- or gun-hand side, especially if you carry the speedloader in a pocket. There are several speedloader carriers on the market. If your snubby is a six-shot, the little belt clip that Ayoob sells is secure, fast, and concealable. (Available from Police Bookshelf, P.O. Box 122, Concord, NH 03301.) Yet another advantage of the Alessi shoulder holster is that it comes with a speedloader pouch.

At this point I need to acknowledge that 9mm and .45 ACP revolvers use full- or half-moon clips, and they are considered by those who use them to be even faster than speedloaders. My impression is that they see little use outside of various competitions. I also need to acknowledge that there are several other methods of using the speedloader. This particular method is probably the most commonly used because it is about the most fumble-proof of the speedloader techniques.

A couple of other considerations: You reload because you *have* to (all rounds have been fired). Or you reload

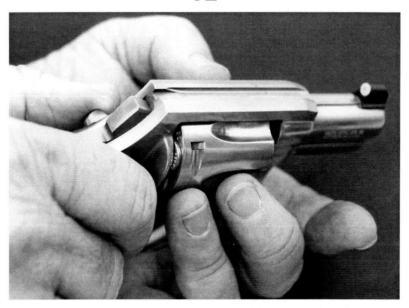

Hand placement to begin the revolver reload sequence.

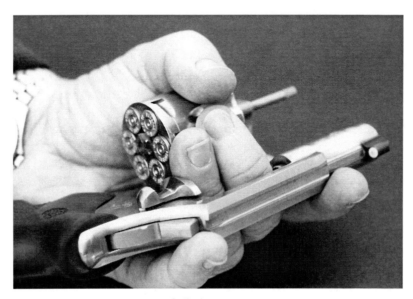

Cylinder open.

Muzzle up.

because you *feel the need* to (your assailant is down and you can't remember how many rounds you've fired). If you *think* you have to reload, you probably do. Remember also that when you reload, your revolver, unlike certain of the pistols, is out of action. You can't fire it. So you should reload behind cover. And finally, the revolver takes more concentration to reload than the pistol. Possibly for this or a variety of other reasons, we all have the tendency to look down at the revolver at about waist level while reloading. This habit causes us to take our eyes off of our assailant or, worse yet, the last place we knew our assailant to be. Adjust this technique, keeping the snubby at chest level so you can see to reload and also keep an eye on the bad guy.

Assuming you are right-handed (left-handers need only read 4, 5, 7, and 8, then proceed to the next section, which is just for you), place the bottom of the trigger guard in the palm of your support or nonfiring hand.

Strike extractor rod sharply with heel of free hand.

Bring revolver into body at chest height, muzzle down.

Focus on two charge holes under your thumb and insert rounds.

As soon as rounds release into the cylinder, drop the speedloader.

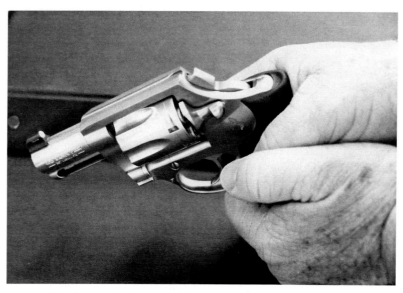

Regrip revolver, close cylinder, and get back in the fight.

Position your fingers as shown in the photo.

Activate the cylinder release and open the cylinder.

Place the elbow of the hand holding the gun on your stomach (not your side). Point the barrel of the snubby straight up. (This keeps the gun about chest level. Don't forget the bad guy!)

Smack the extractor rod with the heel of your free hand. This "spank-the-baby" technique is intended to make up for the snubby's short extractor rod. It forcefully expels the empty shell casings from the cylinder. Don't push the rod and hold it down. Forcefully smack and release because the "smacking" hand now has to grab the speedloader.

Point the barrel down at the ground. (Don't forget about the bad guy. Where is he now?)

You have the speedloader in hand. A helpful hint passed on to me back when we were all pretty sure the earth was flat: Don't attempt to load all five or six rounds (depending on your revolver choice) into all five or six charge holes in the cylinder. Just concentrate on loading two rounds into the two charge holes under your thumb. (The one wrapped around the cylinder) Trust me, the rest will follow. This will help steady you in a low-light situation because you can always see or find your thumb.

Push the speedloader until the rounds are ejected into the charge holes, *and then forget about the speedloader.* I've seen people throw the loader with great gusto at every point on the compass. Don't do this. You're wasting time. Gravity will take care of the empty loader.

Push the revolver grip firmly into the firing hand while at the same time closing the cylinder on the snubby, and you are back in the fight.

If you are left-handed . . .

- Place the bottom of the trigger guard in the palm of your support or nonfiring hand.
- Position your fingers as shown in photo.

- Activate the cylinder release and open the cylinder. (You'll have to decide which is easier, thumb or forefinger.)
- Place the elbow of the hand holding the gun on your stomach (not your side). Point the barrel straight up.
- Smack the extractor rod with the heel of your free hand.
- Grab the speedloader with your free hand.
- Point the barrel at the ground.
- Focus on loading two rounds into the two charge holes directly under your thumb.
- Push the speedloader until the rounds are ejected into the charge holes (see 8 above).
- Push the revolver grip firmly into the firing hand while at the same time closing the cylinder on the snubby, and you are back in the fight.

. . . And if you are injured and have only one hand available, don't give up! There is a solution for that situation too, but it is mighty slow. (This is a situation that is obviously best solved by having a second revolver readily available. Titanium anyone?) You may also find that you need to find a way to have a speedloader available to either hand:

- Open the cylinder and dump the rounds. (This actually works better for me if I can use my left hand.)
- Stick the gun into the waistband and wedge the cylinder open.
- Grab speedloader and reload.
- Close cylinder, grab gun, and get back into the fight.

SHELL CASING UNDER THE EXTRACTOR

This is a problem that may occur with the 4-inch-barreled revolver. It usually occurs during the rapid reloading procedure when you push the extractor rod to eject the spent shells. (Another reason for the "spank-the-baby" method—it seems to eliminate this problem.) It has happened during gunfights and resulted in the death of at least one officer that I am aware of. Shortly after this incident, a California company (if memory serves) came out with a collar that you could put over the extractor rod of the 4-inch revolver, which shortened the extractor rod's stroke, thus eliminating the problem. I don't recall ever seeing it happen with the 2-inch revolver, but just in case . . . the offending cartridge is easily removed with a ballpoint pen. Massad Ayoob's Dejammer also clears this problem up handily.

THE ADMINISTRATIVE RELOAD

You may have unloaded your revolver to clean it, for example, and now you have to put those five or six loose rounds back into the gun. Or you have been doing some dry-fire practice. In this instance I suggest that you reload by hand, one at a time. Do NOT use the speedloader. (In fact, if you confine *all* of your speedloader practice to the range, you will go a long way toward reducing the possibility of a negligent discharge.) This will help condition your mind to the fighting reload response (load quick and get back in the fight) as opposed to the administrative reload response (load the handgun and put it directly into the holster or a safe storage device if you intend to store it loaded). Loading the rounds one at a time forces you to *slow down and think about what you are doing.* As with the speedloader, always load the charge hole under your thumb and rotate the cylinder to bring a fresh charge hole under your thumb. To force yourself to *really* concentrate on what you are doing, rotate the cylinder *opposite* the way it normally turns when the gun is fired.

Before the speedloader era, when all reloading was done from dump pouches or belt loops, this technique was taught to deal with the possibility of a situation in which an officer has to reload during a gunfight and before he can finish doing so he has to close a partially loaded cylinder and engage his assailant. By rotating the cylinder opposite the way it normally turns, you will just about guarantee that you will be able to fire the partially loaded snubby. I suggest it here as a safety measure because it forces you to *think about what you are doing.* It makes you *think* tactically even when the situation doesn't call for it. The administrative reload process (load by hand one at a time, rotate the cylinder counter to the way it turns normally), then, is intended to remind you that you are "going hot." With practice, it will force you to consciously pay attention to what you are doing and why. It will force you to remind yourself that you cannot and must not close the cylinder and bring the gun up one more time for that last shot at that target you've got taped to the door of the closet in your bedroom . . .

PART

THE TACTICS
AND TRAINING

Intro to Tactics

BEFORE WE GET INTO SNUBBY TACTICS, I need to remind everyone that this book is intended to complement *Defensive Living*. Thus, a lot of essential info on awareness, danger signs, the force continuum, legal aspects of deadly force, and so on will not be included here. *The Snubby Revolver* is intended to highlight the virtues of the snub-nose revolver and the tactical strengths it brings to the use-of-force requirement in a comprehensive personal protection plan.

The greatest asset of the 2-inch five- (or six-) shot revolver (in my opinion) is that it allows us to be armed when we otherwise might not be. Like the pocketknife, it may not be the best tool for the job, but it is the one we are most likely to have with us all the time. In this role it will almost always be carried concealed. This defines the snubby's second greatest asset: it affords you the element of surprise, and surprise is one of the ingredients of a winning plan. The surprise factor may only last for a couple of heartbeats, just time enough to allow you to do what you have to do in order to gain tactical dominance over the situation.

Although no two gunfights are alike, it seems to me that the little revolver is always present in the worst-case last-ditch scenarios. Movement is restricted, cover is not available, and if you don't do something *right now*, your situation is going to rapidly get a whole lot worse. You will not have this window of opportunity again. NOTE: The following incident happened to NYPD Lt. Adam Kasanof, who described the events during an "Off-Duty Officer Survival" seminar he gave at the 1994 ASLET conference.

• • •

The police officer was off-duty and enjoying the first day of a well-earned vacation. He was in civilian attire and had a Colt Detective Special handily stashed in the pocket of his winter coat. While seated on a subway train, he was accosted by two men. One of them had a handgun and the other had a knife. They sat down, one on either side of him, and the one with the pistol ordered him to hand over his money. The officer reached into his pocket and got a firm grip on his revolver. As he drew the Detective Special, he grabbed the gunman's wrist, knocked the pistol aside, and fired a single shot. As his assailant rolled off of the seat and onto the floor, the officer turned and fired a shot at the knife wielder, who was now running toward the subway door.

• • •

The off-duty police officer was working as a cab driver to make extra money to support his growing family. He was left-handed; thus his Chiefs Special hung in a shoulder holster under his right arm. The fare he had just picked up was sitting in the right rear of the cab. He produced a handgun and demanded money from the driver of the cab. The officer drew the revolver and fired through the seat. The robber never saw the gun that killed him.

Are You Ready? Part I

EVERY ONCE IN A WHILE you need to take a break, step back, and see how you're doing. This is especially so when we're talking personal security preparedness and it goes double when we add the handgun to the equation.

When I first did this column for Combat Handguns, it was to help people decide which handgun was best for them. It was also my personal account of why I ended up choosing the snubby. Since you've probably already made your handgun choices, I wanted readers of this book to use these incidents more as a self-check on training and mind-set.

The incident analysis is helpful to us because it has the advantage of 20/20 hindsight. It is harsh, brutal, uncompromising. It gives you the "no spin" of reality. The really good news in all of this is that learning from the experience of others is pain-free.

88

INCIDENT ANALYSIS

All of the following incidents but one are discussed in the book, but I will outline them again here so you don't have to look them up. You may note as you read the incident and then the lessons learned that the actual encounter (reality) bears little resemblance to any of the training you've had. I have a simple explanation for this: Most of our training deals with close quarters combat (CQC) technique. We can use verbal commands, gain distance, seek cover. We have the time and distance to apply tactics. However very little of our firearms training deals with extreme close quarters combat (ECQC). In extreme close quarters, we do not have the time and distance to apply tactics. We are fighting with our hands, a knife, a handgun, our training, and our mind-set. These are the dynamics of deadly force encounters most common to the legally armed citizen and they also include the majority of assaults on police officers.

In our book Defensive Living, Dave Spaulding and I discuss willingness, the "Survivor's Attitude" and the promise to yourself to never ever give up once the fight begins. But they are just words on paper. The incidents you are about to read and the ones that follow in Are You Ready? #2 will bring these words to life. These are your/my worst nightmare, in-your-face, lethal assaults that take place from about 3 yards to contact.

The Applegate Incident (single assailant)

As we have described in an earlier chapter, Colonel Applegate, while working in Mexico was attacked by a machete-wielding campesino. Applegate was carrying a five-shot .38 S&W Hammerless. He hit his attacker with all five shots with no effect. Applegate's companion was carrying a Colt 1911 and he was able to bring hostilities to a halt.

Learning Points: This is an excellent incident to work with because it is so easy to visualize, and it gets right to the heart of the defensive handgun's role as a close-range fight stopper. What handgun do you want to be carrying concealed if attacked suddenly at close quarters by someone armed with a long knife? Where do you want to carry your handgun so you can quickly get it into action? What sort of ammo do you want to have in this handgun? Are you going to carry your choice faithfully, on your person, even in hot summer weather? For me this incident establishes the power floor for the defensive handgun at .38 special and 9mm. It helps you to see with startling clarity whether you should grab for the reload or the backup gun. And it also lets you ask yourself, "Is my vision going to be on the front sight of my handgun or glued to the threat?"

The Carjacking (single assailant)

I have two cases in which the driver of the vehicle is in the car with a carjacker who is holding a gun on him or her. Both drivers had .38 special snubbies. One was able to kill the carjacker and the other got shot while trying to draw her revolver.

Learning Points: Take all the necessary precautions to make sure a carjacker cannot get into the car with you (See the chapters on Carjacking Countermeasures). Maybe a disarm would be the fastest response in this situation—have you ever practiced one in a car? In both cases the drivers drew, or attempted to draw, looking down the barrel of a gun. Figure you are seated in the car behind the steering wheel, your handgun is concealed, and you may be wearing your seatbelt. Major opportunities here for a poor grip on the weapon as you draw (which may make your auto pistol a single shot), having to fire one-handed and having to fire with the gun below eye level. This may also cause you to rethink carrying a ported gun if it is going to be below eye level and close to your body when you fire.

The Mugger's Hold (single assailant)

The problem in this case is that your assailant has attacked you from behind. He has a gun at your head or a knife at your throat, and is dragging you into an alley. In the case I have, the assailant had a female officer face down on the ground and he was choking her with her baton. She resolved the situation with a 4-inch S&W Model 15.

Learning Points: While struggling for air you need to draw your handgun, jam it against the person behind you, and pull the trigger until your assailant gets the message. The big problem here is having the cycle of the semiauto pistol interrupted because the muzzle is pressed hard against your attacker. This is not a firing position you will have practiced at the range. It also raises the question, "When I train with my handgun, do I train to shoot or do I train to fight?"

The Hit (two assailants)

In this case two terrorists attempt to kill an individual as he is unlocking the door to his apartment. He senses that they are behind him and is turning as the shot intended for the back of his head is fired. The round strikes him in the side of the face.

Learning Points: Shot in the face at close range, do you have the "Survivor's Attitude" that, against all odds, will keep you in the fight? Can you get to your handgun and deal with your two armed attackers who are barely an arm's length away? Here we have yet another case in which you will probably not be able to bring the handgun to eye level.

The Kidnapping (3 assailants plus??)

As he was leaving his apartment one morning to go to work, three armed terrorists approached a colleague of mine (who was not armed), grabbed him, threw him into the back seat of a car, then sped away. There was probably a backup vehicle with extra muscle and guns nearby.

Learning Points: This one raises a whole host of issues which are not easily considered in writing, issues that you need to have thought through and come to terms with if you are going to live and work in this type of environment.

We'll assume you've done this. You are confronted by three armed kidnappers running at you. They are almost close enough to grab you. The only window of opportunity you have is that if they wanted you dead they'd already be firing. They are expecting you to comply. They are not expecting you to resist. They don't want to attract a lot of attention to themselves. So your job in the next few seconds is to give a whole new meaning to the term "explosive, violent counterattack." You need to quickly create "hell in a very small place" and by the time these three realize you aren't complying, they are dead or dying. Now you only have the backup car left to deal with?! Pretty tall order for the man and the gun. The big learning point here is that you want to do everything possible, every day, while working in a country with a high terrorist threat, to avoid finding yourself in this situation.

• • •

Finally, you have probably noted there was no time for a malfunction clearance or a reload in these situations, another distinction between CQC and ECQC. ECQC places full and unforgiving emphasis on your being able to quickly access your handgun, get it into action, and fire rapidly and with combat accuracy. Are you ready?

Personal Security Equipment

A LOT OF THE TRAINING AVAILABLE to the armed citizen at the "name" schools tends to exclusively address the firearm, though some may offer a separate course on self-defense with the knife or a class on the use of OC spray. You will have to do some looking to find a school that offers a program that combines or integrates all of the force continuum skills in force-on-force scenarios. All of the schools that I discuss in the book—Options for Personal Security, Tactical Defense Institute, Northeastern Tactical Schools, and Gunfighters Ltd.—have versions of integrated training courses you might find useful.

This is where you want your personal defensive skill level to be, and such integrated training is especially useful in helping you determine what personal security equipment (PSE) you really need. (If you read enough books and magazines on the subject, and took their advice, you'd

Most people would consider this the basics, with or without a handgun.

leave home each morning looking like a combat infantry-man—you'd be the envy of every street cop in your neighborhood, and they'd probably consider calling on you if the SWAT team got into a jam.) The vital question, "What do I really need?" is one only you can answer, but a little help would be nice.

Personally, I'd like to see something on the order of a two-day seminar that would help a participant select suitable equipment and then would put him into role-play situations that would test his reactions to see if he selects the appropriate tool for the threat and uses it effectively. This course would consist of short, focused presentations on the following subjects with time for some hands-on practice where appropriate so you could make up your mind on whether or not, for example, you really need a collapsible baton. To set the stage:

- *Threat Awareness (criminal):* This is the heart of personal security. Training in this category should include learning to identify a threat, learning how to avoid placing yourself at risk, and learning the danger signs of an imminent assault.
- *Threat Awareness (terrorism):* Unfortunately, today this is a concern we all share. We each need to know those signs and indicators that can tell us we are looking at possible terrorist surveillance or casing at or near subways, financial institutions, power plants, dams, and the like. We need to better understand the crucial role we play in detecting and reporting possible terrorist activities in the United States.
- *Combat Mind-Set:* How do you put on your game face or access your fighting state? How do you go from Condition Yellow to Condition Red in the shortest possible time? How do you condition yourself to do what needs to be done?

These classes would then be followed by a series of mini-seminars that would cover the following subjects concerning PSE:

- *Communications:* This would teach the importance of verbal skills—what to say, how to say it, when to say it, what to do with your hands. In this class you will reinforce how to access your fighting state when the hands come up so that your body language (stance and facial expression) instantly communicates to your assailant that you refuse to be a victim. Also, here we discuss the importance of the cell phone.
- *Unarmed Defense:* Certainly not everyone's favorite scenario, but you may be offered no choice. You have no OC, no knife, no gun and you need to do something to get away from someone—you need to create distance to allow you to access and use the appropriate tool. So, some simple moves should be demonstrated and prac-

ticed, such as stepping back and/or getting off the line of attack. Your best solution may be to run, but he is between you and the only exit. Your hands are already up so you can quickly shove, slap, or eye gouge. Training should teach you to recognize the danger signs and respond to an attack at reactionary gap distances (6 feet to contact), which is the severest test for equipment and technique.

- *OC Spray:* It is here that we can state a rule. *A rule is something that you need to understand will cost you if you choose to violate it.* The rule is that if you carry a firearm you must also carry a less-than-lethal tool such as OC spray or a collapsible baton. OC's big advantage over other intermediate use-of-force weapons is that it allows you to put the brakes on an attacker without having to lay hands on him or giving him the opportunity to come into contact with you. Since there are many brands of OC, the most effective ones should be discussed here as well. As far as I know, one of the top contenders these days is the Fox Labs OC. One of my cop friends says if you're ever hit in the face with this stuff, it makes you want to pull your face off and throw it away! This leads us to a discussion on how we can fight through the effects of OC if we have to.

- *Flashlight:* We've probably seen more advances in flashlight technology in recent years than most any other PSE item. They just keep getting smaller and lighter and more powerful. They also offer a multi-use advantage. In addition to being used to help us see, the powerful beam can be used as a momentary distraction to buy us some time and the flashlight can be used against your attacker much like the kubotan. Suitable types and their use should be discussed and practiced here.

- *Collapsible Baton:* Standard equipment for American law enforcement, it is simple to use and can be extremely effective. It also gives you a tool that permits you to quickly break into or out of a vehicle in an emergency. (But we haven't even gotten to the handgun yet and my pockets are already full. I clank when I walk!)

- *Knives:* The folding knife with the pocket clip is all the rage these days. But is it for you? That's what we're here to find out. Is the neck knife a better option? You can reach it with either hand, and it won't fold up on your fingers in a fight. And it can be had with two sharp edges instead of one. Both types, folder or neck fixed blade, can cut you or someone else out of a jammed seat belt. Both can serve as real discouragers if someone tries to take your handgun away from you. If you prefer the folder, does the thumb hole offer any advantages over the thumb stud or vice versa? And in this session we need to have a frank discussion about AIDS and knife fighting, field first aid, emergency room procedures, and so forth.

- *Handguns:* Just as I'm about to collapse under the weight of all these goodies, we get to the handgun. And while I'm trying to catch my breath, I hear another rule: If you carry a handgun you should carry at least one reload or a second gun. In this mini-seminar we discuss handgun selection, holster, and ammo. I would suspect that airweight snubbies, such as those available from S&W and Taurus, and lightweight pocket autos, such as the Kel-Tec, are probably starting to look real attractive about now. Here we will have a chance to handle and shoot a variety of small handguns, pistols, and revolvers, so you can decide which works best for you. As for ammo, as I discuss elsewhere in the book, I think the little guns really benefit from MagSafe. If you are carrying a snub-nose .38 Special, the .380, a .32 ACP or a .25 auto and they are not stuffed with MagSafe, "You got some 'splainin' to do."

- *Vehicles:* Well at least the car can help me lug all this stuff around. I have sort of a hip-pocket course I've taught in the past that the students named "Carjacking Countermeasures for Soccer Moms." It is simple, effective, can be taught and practiced in a parking lot and best of all, you can use your own car.

- *Improvised Weapons:* At the end of the day, we may make great choices for what we want to have with us, but as soon as we board an airplane or change jurisdictions, we may have to leave most if not all of our tools behind. We are especially vulnerable on the airplane. Hence, a class on improvised weapons. We often have something close at hand, if we use a little imagination, that can help us out of a tight spot. Newspapers, magazines, pens and pencils, belts, pepper, coffee, hair spray, key rings—well you get the idea.

This would take care of the PSE. Before moving on to the role-play exercises, I would like to do two other classroom sessions. The first class would be with a lawyer who would cover the realities of the law and a citizen's right to use of force. He'd explain how you can do everything right and still end up in court. This course would teach you what to expect if you are involved in a shooting, how to choose a lawyer, what you can expect in court, and so forth.

And the second class—to get the creative thought processes up and running—would be studies of actual incidents, with the emphasis on what worked. I have special favorites here, my latest being the 66-year-old woman who used a .38 Special revolver to defend herself and her granddaughter from an intruder. She had purchased the handgun for personal protection and had taken a course in how to use it.

My wife caught it on the news and videotaped the interview with this woman. During the incident, the homeowner kept her .38 trained on the intruder while her granddaughter was on the phone with the police dispatcher. They played the 911 call on the show and I couldn't stop cheering! This lady displayed the courage and fighting spirit of our young warriors currently taking the fight to the enemy in Iraq and Afghanistan. I don't know the particulars on the gun and ammo she used, but this woman's actions serve as a superb reminder that "Guns don't win gunfights, people do." The point of course being that in the end, good equipment and good training are important, but what usually wins a confrontation between an armed, alert, and determined citizen faced with a predator cannot be purchased with money.

FLASHLIGHT UPDATE

The small, powerful tactical flashlight certainly needs no introduction here. The latest news regarding these lights as this is written is the addition of the strobe capability that several of them now offer. I have very limited use with one of these strobe lights, so I talked with Lou Chiodo about them. Chiodo is offering one called the Lightsaver LS 162 (which offers a constant white light or the strobe depending on how you depress the end cap button), and I suspect he not only knows as much as anybody else about them but can explain it in easy-to-understand language. The info provided here is extracted from an article Chiodo recently had published in the Great Lakes Self Defense Association newsletter. (Note: You can go to his Web site to see the complete article).

BRIGHTEN UP YOUR NIGHT

So what is the big deal about having a strobe function on a flashlight? Well, we have discussed the goal of "attacking" your opponent's eyes to better your chances of winning the encounter. The strobe will give you some added advantage in certain situations that will help you accomplish your objective. Let's discuss this issue.

First off, please understand that the ability to have a strobe feature in your flashlight is not the end-all cure for

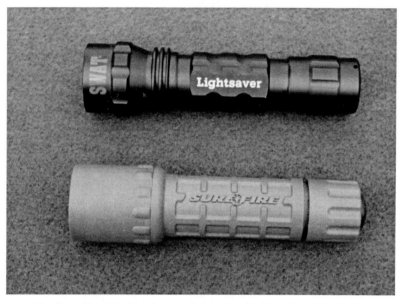

The SureFire Nitrolon (bottom) shown with Lou Chiodo's SWAT Lightsaver LS 162 Blitzer.

The SWAT Lightsaver LS 162 Blitzer with SureFire's E2E Executive Elite. The Lightsaver offers the popular strobe feature.

all nighttime/low-light tactical problems. It is a tool that can be used to help us win. Generally speaking, if there is enough ambient lighting present so that you can still somewhat see the environment/opponent, then the effects of the strobe will be somewhat diminished. The strobe really comes into its own when you are in lighting conditions where it is extremely dark and ambient light doesn't allow much view of the environment. In order to maximize the effects of a strobe feature, the darker, the better. The reason is simple: If your opponent has to use his night vision to attempt to see you, his eyes are working via his rod cells (much like his side vision during daylight). His forward vision has been reduced to next to nothing because of the darkness and then the strobe bombards what is remaining of his forward vision and if he looks towards the light source it only gets worse at the rate of approximately 7 times per second (the strobe flash frequency). If he turns his head to try to see you, his rod cells get blasted. This is a good thing for the good guys. Also, if you are moving, the strobe is allowing what little information his eyes are transmitting to the brain to be distorted and more confusing to analyze. Meanwhile if you combine that with movement in a close-quarters engagement, it will be more difficult for your opponent to track you.

In the context of use of artificial light in a tactical/personal defense environment, our objective is to enhance our vision and degrade our adversary's vision. What is good for us must become bad for our adversary.

• • •

You needed to read Chiodo's explanation of the strobe's effectiveness to really appreciate this next quote from him, taken from our correspondence, which sums up the strobe in 75 words or less. "I have never seen anything that messes with the eyes like the strobe. It is a fighting tool. It can help the officer get inside the subject's OODA [observe, ori-

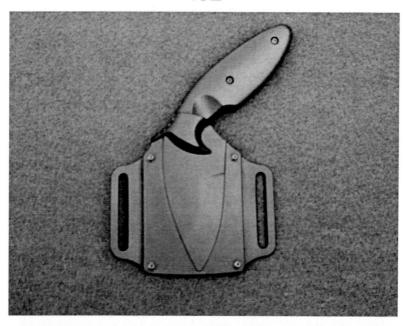

John Benner's popular TDI knife.

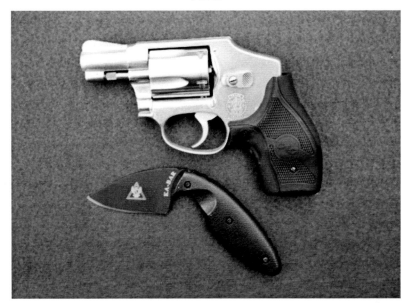

As with the revolver, simply draw and punch.

ent, decide, act] loop. If the subject is at the top of the loop when the officer uses the strobe and the officer is at Act, the strobe disorients the subject long enough to buy the officer the extra time he needs to control the situation." According to Chioda, this is what he is learning from field reports of officers using the strobe.

KNIFE UPDATE

For those of you who are still trying to find the knife and the appropriate training that is right for you, John Benner, founder of the Tactical Defense Institute, may have the solution to both of these issues. Benner, in collaboration with KA-BAR knives, has developed the TDI knife, a small, fixed-blade knife specifically designed for law enforcement officers for weapon retention.

There is an awful lot of new "kit" on today's market.

Some of it works, some of it doesn't. If you carry a handgun you also carry the risk of having someone try to take it away from you. You know that handgun retention skills require strength, leverage, and practice. We all know there is no free lunch, but Benner's TDI knife comes close. If you can supply the fighting spirit and the willingness, this simple, effective weapon gives us average guys and gals a realistic chance of winning a life-or-death struggle.

The knife handle is at an angle to the blade so it sits in your hand like a snubby. It is worn on the side of your body opposite your gun so that it is available to your weak hand. And drawing and using the knife is the same technique you use for drawing and firing the snubby with one hand. You can put all of your energy and body weight behind a punch with this knife using a locked wrist. If all you can remember at the moment is to punch the blade straight forward, just like you do with your handgun, you're good to go. Just keep punching until your assailant gets the message. As long as you are able to make a fist you should be able to hang onto this knife and stay in the fight. And the handle to blade angle helps to keep your hand from overriding the handle and ending up holding the blade, another problem you can encounter with the folder.

I asked Benner where he thought this fit in with the technique of a backup gun in the officer's front pocket to deal with the same problem. He said the TDI gives you another option if you can't get to your pocket revolver and, under some circumstances, it may be faster into action than the handgun. His test consists of having the student draw the knife and pop a balloon. With the folder this can take from 1.5 seconds to as much as 10, depending on the student's skill level. With the TDI knife it takes about a second.

Benner also told me about another advantage the knife could give you in a close-quarters fight that turns lethal: "In an extreme close-quarters environment where the firearm is not in the hand—yet—it may be appropriate to go for the knife over the gun. The probable reason for doing that is because you are against an opponent that is larger or stronger and you feel your only option is to escalate to deadly force to save your life. If you escalate with the pistol/revolver (better with the snubby since it does not have as much room for purchase) you very well may get your handgun taken away. It is very difficult to take the knife away (especially the TDI since you have a good, full hand grip from the get go). I just think there is a larger risk of losing the gun than the knife." Sounds like pretty good advice coming from someone who teaches ECQ combatives for a living.

I am not a martial artist or a knife fighter but this is one of those rare examples where the careful attention to detail that went into the TDI design can help you to be all that you can be with very little practice and effort. This is an extremely user friendly knife. If you are interested in a well-designed knife and serious training to go with it, give Benner a call.

Fox Labs International
20752 Miles St. South
Clinton Township, MI 48036-4948
www.foxlabs.net

John Benner
Tactical Defense Institute
2174 Bethany Ridge Rd.
West Union, Ohio 45693
www.tdiohio.com

Maintaining Your Alertness Level

We've all heard the catchy little phrases intended to remind us to stay alert to personal security threats, such as, "Stay Alert! Stay Alive!" and "Beware by Being Aware." The truth is that maintaining a level of alertness intended to help us see a problem in time to deal with it appropriately takes commitment and concentration. The more we practice the easier it gets but, as with maintaining your handgun proficiency, we have to work at it. And it is easy to get lax by being bored, tired, distracted, and so on. In order to combat this over the years I have developed some self-aids that I use to get me focused and to keep me focused when I need to be. Hopefully, you might find these useful if you don't already have some of your own.

I think this is especially critical now because the global War on Terror is exactly that. We are conducting this fight on many fronts, to include right here in America, the home front. Consider the following:

- As this is being written there is another message from Osama bin Laden that the intel community is taking very seriously as the warning for an attack in the near future
- Our borders to the north and south are still not under control
- The FBI believes that we have a foreign terrorist presence in at least 40 states in the United States

It is important that we factor this sort of information into our awareness skills. In addition to paying attention to the danger signs for various street-crime assaults we must now pay attention to what may be indicators of possible terrorist-related activities. We may see this in the form of surveillance/casing or possibly other not-so-obvious preparations for an upcoming attack, such as the recent purchases of untraceable cell phones, as many as 100 at a time, in several major U.S. cities by young Arab males.

The terrorists are here. They live, work, and travel among us, hiding in plain view. And we must not ignore them.

Consider the London tube and bus bombings of 2005 as an example. The city of London has extensive surveillance camera coverage on its subways and buses, possibly the most, and some might say the best, of any major city in the world. In addition, just prior to the attacks, the London Metropolitan Police ran a 30-day terrorist awareness program, "If You Suspect It, Report It," with lots of TV coverage. And yet, the attacks took place. Probably a good example of the observation that, "The good guys have to be right all the time while the bad guys only have to be lucky once."

Which brings up several points we should consider. First is that, while surveillance cameras are helpful, they are still dependent on people to make them effective. The Brits have lots more expertise and have spent more time on this, courtesy of "The Troubles," than we have. Their experience tells us that we need another protective layer between the surveillance cameras and the bad guys. So, point number two, reinforced by the Israeli experience, is that suicide bombers are often stopped short of their destination by an alert public who knows what to look for. In addition, the Israelis also use spotters in key locations—specialized surveillance personnel trained in recognizing and stopping the bombers. They know there is simply no substitute for the "Mark I eyeball." And this brings us to my third point, which is that initial awareness training for the public-at-large must be a live presentation to be effective. We have proven that this will give us better results than reading a book or watching a video on the subject. These are OK for refreshing your skills but not for learning the alertness/awareness basics. And this training must include knowing how and when to make sure we are "switched on."

BASIC ALERTNESS

Switching On

Once you have a grasp of the basics you can switch "on" and "off" at will. Thus, to and from work or anytime you are on the street you need to be switched "on." The trick is that you need to be street-ready before you leave your home or your office. This is often easier said than done (using the home as an example) because one of the kids may be sick, you just had a fight with your spouse, you have an endless supply of bills and a real shortage of cash, and so on. But despite these problems, every morning you still need to leave the house, get into your car, and go to work.

To keep this really simple and thus workable, I use two switches. Col. Cooper told us many years ago, when you put on a gun, you need to go into condition yellow. You need to free up your mind so that it can begin to receive the input you need to pick up and process in order to spot trouble. If you are not carrying a sidearm, a final check is to key your alertness turn-on to switching on your vehicle. When putting your car in drive, do likewise with your awareness.

Question That Which Doesn't Fit

Asking yourself questions about what you are seeing helps you separate what fits from what doesn't. And, equally important, it helps you focus on a person or detail and resolve their behavior or presence. This simple act instantly makes them less of a threat, because now they can't surprise you.

I have discussed this before using the example of kidnap victims who were recovered and debriefed. During the debrief they almost always realized that they had seen indicators of the pre-kidnap preparations as well as some of the players prior to the day they were taken. In some cases they had actually spoken to them! They had simply refused to believe it could happen to them, so they never questioned what they were seeing, even though they were in a high-risk group (wealthy, traveled alone, had no security, established a routine). This allowed their denial mechanism to override their protective awareness capability.

Make It Personal

This is probably another way of saying, "Use what works for you." If you "own it" you're more likely to use it. In my case, it is a mental picture that, although it took place more than 20 years ago, is as vivid today as if it just happened.

During my government service, I was working with a host government unit overseas in a liaison capacity. We were returning to the hotel one evening when they contacted us by radio and asked that we return to the compound. Once there, it was easy to see that everyone was pretty excited—and with good reason. Turns out they had just grabbed a suicide bomber and his vehicle. They took me out back to look at the car and it was absolutely packed with plastic explosives. Frankly, being around explosives makes me plumb nervous, so I was glad when they said we were going to see the driver.

We went upstairs to a holding cell. In the cell was a young man with a shaved head (sometimes this was one of the suicide-bomber preparations, but I didn't know that at the time) wearing coveralls and smoking a cigarette. They ordered him to walk over to the bars so I could see him clearly. I remember thinking that he walked as if he owned the place; he showed no fear at all. And by then he was standing at the bars of the cell, about an arm's length from me and I saw his eyes. And I will never forget them. They were cold, dead, totally devoid of life. If the eyes are the windows to the soul, his was long gone. He looked right through me, and it wasn't until later that I realized I couldn't even see his pupils. To me, the phrase "dead man walking" best describes those eyes.

Anytime I need to recharge my awareness/alertness batteries all I have to do is bring up the image of those soulless eyes. They serve to remind me that someone somewhere right now is plotting to attack this great nation. Consequently, you need to constantly remind yourself that one of the most important, most effective, and least expensive resources your country is now depending on to strengthen our homeland security effort is you and your awareness skills.

Surveillance
Awareness

THE WOMAN HAD A LEGAL restraining order against her estranged husband. For the last several months he had not bothered her at her apartment. She had finally begun to relax a little at work, the only place where she felt truly safe. Several times a day when she took her breaks, she would walk the few short steps from her office building to a nearby set of picnic tables, which was the company's designated smoking area. She knew that cigarettes, like her former husband, were a bad habit she would have to give up. But not today. As she concentrated on lighting the cigarette, the man approached her. While her horrified coworkers looked on, he shot her and then turned the pistol on himself.

• • •

Defensive Living discussed increasing your awareness and the danger signs of an imminent street-crime assault. Now I want to kick it up a notch. Surveillance detection (SD) seems to be one of those terms, like terrorism, that everybody defines differently. For our purposes, SD is what a lone individual can do to determine whether he or she is being watched. It is one of the components of an intelligence officer's tradecraft, an essential skill for the protective operations specialist and, lest we forget, commonly used by serious criminals. SD is an art form and can get pretty complicated. Surveillance awareness (SA), on the other hand, is the intro to SD and is useful to us all because it is simple and straightforward. It helps us sort out the known from the unknown, the familiar from the unfamiliar, especially in the two areas we spend most of our waking hours, our home and our workplace. Once mastered, it allows you to deal with a variety of threats, such as stalking, carjacking, and kidnapping. It can keep you out of trouble by serving as an early warning of the fact that someone is interested in you. It is the weakest link in the planning phase of a criminal act. Someone may watch you for months (kidnapping) or for seconds (carjacking). But in either case, for violent crimes against your person to take place, the bad guys have to get close to you, or let you get close to them. So (to paraphrase the bomb tech's sage advice, "If you can see the bomb, the bomb can see you"), if the bad guys can see you, you can see the bad guys.

For most of us to get good at any skill, we need training followed by lots of practice. As with any type of awareness training, the tough part about SA is not the technique but the concentration that it requires. You must constantly pay attention to what is going on around you, and you must not ignore what you see. (Sounds a lot like Condition Yellow, doesn't it?) People untrained in SA often see the threat but attach no significance to it and fail to catalog it properly. (Sounds a lot like Condition White, doesn't it?) So, for SA to work for you, you need to know WHAT to look for, WHERE to look for it, and WHAT to do about it.

So let's say you are under a real or perceived threat. Consequently, you have decided to ramp up your personal security habits. You are varying your routes and times to and from work. You have a choice of three routes, and you drive a different one each day. Let's say these routes allow you to maintain a fairly constant speed, so it would take some work for someone to stop you (speed is your ally). You still must contend with the roadways near your home or office, because they usually force you to come and go pretty much the same way all the time, and you have to slow down or stop frequently. Here you need to take advantage of what appears to be a disadvantage. Guess who's going to be there with you? Sure, because they want you to make their job easy. So you are always watchful, but you are extra alert near these two areas.

To determine WHAT to look for, you need to understand a couple of things about surveillance (and again, everybody's definitions are different). For our purposes, we'll concern ourselves with three types of surveillance:

- *Foot* (this is the stuff you see in all the private eye shows, where someone follows someone on foot).
- *Fixed* (the person watching you is not moving and thus pretty tough to spot).
- *Mobile* (the surveillants are in a vehicle following you). For example, if the surveillants are in a van, parked so as to be able to watch you leave for work in the morning, they would be considered fixed surveillance. If they use the van to follow you to work they would be considered mobile surveillance.

Some examples of WHERE you want to focus your attention near your home, near your work, while in your vehicle, or while approaching your vehicle would be parked cars containing people, park benches, phone booths, bus stops, and restaurants with outside eating facilities. Now, out of all the people we are likely to see, how do we tell who is interested in us? We have three indicators:

- Location
- Correlation
- Demeanor

Let's look at an example: The CEO of a small corporation had taken a personal security course at his wife's insistence. The training taught him the value of SA. On his way to work after the training, he began to notice a man sitting on a bench (fixed surveillance) at a bus stop near his home. Something about his clothing just didn't fit the neighborhood (*location*). Over a period of several days, each morning as the CEO left for work he noticed the man was always there (*correlation*).

Since his house overlooked the bus stop, one morning the CEO stayed home and watched the man from a second floor window. Once the surveillant realized the CEO was not leaving for work at the usual time, he became visibly nervous and kept glancing at his watch. Finally, he got up from the bench and walked over to a bicycle hidden in some bushes. The man got on the bike and pedaled away (*demeanor*).

Faced with a similar situation, what do you do? *Take action!* Tell someone who can follow up on what you've seen. Do not ignore this series of events. In this case the CEO called the police, who arrested the man and uncovered a kidnap plot.

POP QUIZ: You have one person watching your home and two people following you to work. They are checking to see if you are a hard target or an easy one. How many of these people do you need to spot to know you've got a problem?

ANSWER: Just one.

Basic Tactics

ACCEPT THE FACT THAT IT *CAN* HAPPEN TO YOU!

BE PREPARED!

HAVE A PLAN!

TAKE ACTION!
(DON'T FORGET THAT TAKING ACTION MAY MEAN
BEING THE VERY BEST WITNESS YOU CAN BE WHILE
GIVING UP YOUR CAR OR WALLET.)

To successfully manage an armed confrontation requires a working blend of mind-set, tactics, and shooting skill that you must be able to apply under extreme stress. In theory, these three are equally important. In reality, I think mind-set and tactics weigh in much heavier in the equation for a lot of reasons—not the least of which is the fact that they often keep you from having to resort to firing your weapon. Poor marksmanship and lousy shot placement can get you into trouble. But improper or nonexistent mind-set and failure to use sound tactics collectively cause more grief in the majority of deadly force encounters. Consider the following errors, which quite often snatch defeat from the jaws of victory: failure to correctly assess the threat, failure to control the subject, failure to watch the hands, failure to use cover, failure to shoot soon enough. Obviously, then, failure to hit and failure to stop are often the end result of a chain of events that began when you either lost control of the situation (tactics) or never saw it coming (awareness, one of the components of mind-set). In fact, basic lethal force tactics (distance and cover) take into account the marginal stopping power of the handgun and the difficulties of shooting a handgun accurately under stress.

Further, basic tactics that enable you to manage an armed confrontation have a couple of distinctive characteristics. One is that if you don't adhere to them your chances of being injured (or worse) are virtually guaranteed. Second, like the firing stroke, they must be a conditioned response. If you start behind the curve and you have to stop and think about what you are going to do, you'll never catch up.

I like to tie tactics to the Color Code. As your awareness level goes up, so does your tactical response. This also helps to ensure that the tactics are taught in the proper mental state. Condition Red tactics, for example, need to be practiced under conditions that simulate a gunfight. So consider the following list as more than simple tactical procedures; think of it as a tactical thought process to assist you as you mentally race from Yellow to Orange to Red. While gunhandling and shooting skills are blended or used together with tactical skills in practice, I try, where possible, to distinguish them. Finally, it is understood that you may not have time to do all of these tactical procedures by the numbers.

1) Realize that you have a problem.
2) Make effective use of available time.
   a. Breathe.
   b. Quickly assess the situation.
   c. Make a hasty plan. (What are my goals?
      What are my options?)
3) Use clear verbal commands.
4) Identify and use cover.
5) Gain and maintain distance.
6) Know where the exits are.
7) *If* shots have been fired and your opponent is down
   or gone . . .
   a. Do a quick "+1" scan (see below) to make sure
      there are no more bad guys.
   b. Reload.
   c. Check yourself to make sure you have not been hit.
8) Call the cops as soon as possible.

Realize that you have a problem: This is your situational awareness at work. You pick up cues or danger signs that signal that you have a problem. You go from Condition Yellow (generally alert) to Condition Orange (specifically alert). Your training, mental preparation, and mental conditioning have prepared you to deal with this eventuality.

Make effective use of available time: Critical incidents usually take place within a very short timeframe. They are extremely unforgiving and leave little to no room for error. If you have any time at all to make a hasty plan, take full advantage. Failing to make a plan just adds to the confusion and creates more room for mental stalling. Try to slow the clock. Controlling the clock is easier to do than beating the clock. Don't forget to breathe.

Use clear, concise verbal commands (if time allows): Don't just point your trusty snubby at someone and say nothing. Take charge. Tell him what you want him to do.

Keep your commands short. Don't exchange dialogue with the individual.

Identify and use cover: Again, this only applies if time allows. There are times when moving to cover is simply not an option. Given the time-distance factor, your best/only option may be to shoot—*NOW*. Know what cover is, because if you have to move you want to move from concealment to cover or from cover to better cover.

Gain and maintain distance: Distance + Cover = High Probability for Survival. Where handguns are involved, anything past 21 feet greatly increases your chances of not being hit.

Know where the exits are: See Chapter 12.

IF shots have been fired: Do a quick "+1" scan to make sure there is no additional threat, reload, then do your quick check to make sure you're OK.

Call the cops: Massad Ayoob makes the point in his LFI-I class that the sooner you call the police, the better your chances of establishing yourself as the victim.

Derringer Tactics

TO ME, THE FIVE-SHOT SNUBBY is the modern-day equivalent of the riverboat gambler's derringer. Like the derringer, it is light and small enough to always have with you. But, also like the derringer, it and the word firepower should not be used in the same sentence (without including the phrase "lack of"). Effective confrontation management with the five-shot revolver places a premium on strong tactical skills.

What I want to discuss here is an extension of the previous chapter on tactics. Those are the basics. These are specifically for the pocket revolver—things you might wish to consider before you find yourself in a situation where your keen intellect, sparkling wit, and track and field skills are all required to offset the fact that you are mighty light on firepower.

1) Plan A—Don't forget that your best tactic may be to avoid the fight if possible. If the little .38 Special is your only

The Ayoob Dejammer with keys can be used as a flail.

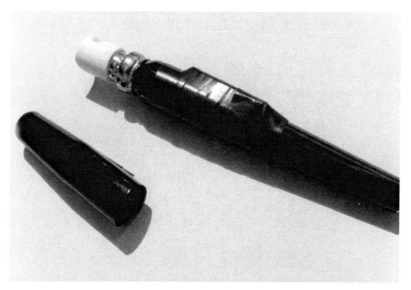

OC spray is a great deterrent when it works; this OC pen has a match-
stick taped to the barrel of the pen so that you can tell by feel that the
spray is pointed in the right direction.

The snubby is a natural for the Discreet Ready carry.

armament, maybe you should give strong consideration to Plan B.

2) Plan B—Always have an exit. Can you run away to fight another day?

3) Give yourself some tactical flexibility. In addition to your choice of "derringer," carry a less-than-lethal-force option such as pepper spray or a flail. Don't put yourself in the position of having to use a hammer when all you really needed was a screwdriver.

4) The plan that looks workable when you're by yourself is probably not the one you want when with your family.

5) Use surprise to your advantage. By the time your opponent learns you are armed, it should be too late for him to react.

6) The little Centennial, properly positioned, lends itself to discreet access. You can have your hand on the gun without your opponent's knowing it. Crossdraw or shoulder holsters (while seated) or pocket holsters (while standing) offer good examples of this.

7) The small revolver also permits you to use a Discreet Ready (e.g., the gun in the pocket of your windbreaker or the gun in your hand with a coat thrown over your arm). The gun is in your hand and pointed at your assailant without his knowing it.

8) In a confrontation, remember the "+1" rule: There is always the possibility of the bad guys you see having with them "+1" you don't. So protect your back. You will not be able to watch everyone/everywhere at once. As early as possible, get something solid behind you (e.g., a wall, a car, etc.).

9) Practice-Practice-Practice. You should be a serious threat to a target the size of an 8 1/2 x 11 sheet of typing paper from arm's length to 21 feet.

10) Always carry two guns or at least one speedloader.

11) Select ammo that maximizes the performance of the short-barreled .38 Special but remember, sexy ammo will not make up for lousy shot placement. Refer to #9 above?

12) Don't eat at anyplace called "Mom's." Never play cards with anyone named "Doc."

Always Have an Exit

WE SEE IT IN THE NEWS all too frequently: people are trapped (or believe themselves to be trapped) in restaurants, office buildings, schools, and hotels. Maybe the restaurant they're in is being robbed, or perhaps their workplace is being shot up by a lone crazed gunman. What I'm going to consider in this chapter are the tactics you must employ in order to safely get out of a building containing a threat. Please note that your home is not included in the list of possible problem areas. Circumstances and situations may dictate otherwise, but as a general rule I am not advocating these tactics for home defense scenarios. Anyone who enters your house intent on doing harm to you and yours should be dealt with accordingly. One way or another, he leaves. You don't. 'Nuff said.

Common sense dictates that any time we are in a building we should always have an exit plan. Know where the exits are. Know what you can use for cover as you move to the exit. If something happens that causes you to activate your exit plan, do a quick assessment of the threat (don't forget to breathe) and then act. To quote John Farnam's sage advice, "Don't be a gawking spectator. Get out at the first sign of trouble. Don't panic and don't dither. Take decisive action immediately. Anything is better than sitting there exclaiming, 'What should we do'?"

For instance: We've all heard that the best place to sit in a restaurant is at a table at the back of the dining area. This vantage point allows you to watch everything that is going on. You can cover the entrance while keeping your back to the wall. My buddy Dave Spaulding advocates sitting close to an exit. If something happens you're out the door before the situation develops. I know a father and daughter who beat the terrorist bombing of a fast food place by doing exactly that. The bad guys looked out of place. Something didn't feel right. As quickly as they entered through one door, dad and daughter left through another. Less than a minute later the building was in ruins.

There are two schools of thought as to *how* you should exit. (Again, since the emphasis of this book is on the private citizen, all of this presumes you are in civilian attire, hence more or less invisible.) One is to move quickly but in a nonalerting manner while scanning.

The other is to run for your life, literally. This is a decision only you can make when you do your quick assessment of the situation prior to implementing your exit plan. Perhaps your feet are ready to fly, but you note that the bad guys are *between* you and the nearest exit. Time for plan B. . . Or by the time you realize what is going on, everybody is running to the exit. You have no choice. If caught up in a panicked crowd, go with the flow while trying to work your way toward the edge of the frenzy. Especially if you have to negotiate stairs. Being at the edge of this human freight train may allow you to gain cover until the "train" roars past. Then you make your way down the stairs. So running may be the correct (only) answer and the fastest way out. It may also induce panic, clouding your ability to make good decisions quickly. And it may be alerting at a time when you really wish to be invisible.

The "scan while moving" option assumes you know what is happening before most everyone else does. Or you're already moving while everyone else is trying to decide what to do. It is slower than running but allows you to look before you leap, think clearly and quickly, keep your balance, and so on (a couple of departures from the norm). This is *not* a building search or room clearing technique. This is simply watching where you put your foot down and checking the corners as you move. You are not stopping to do a textbook clearing exercise. You check the angles but stay constantly in motion. Anyone watching you would probably not notice anything unusual about your actions.

You are trying to avoid being surprised by the threat or mistaken as the threat. Use all of your senses. Don't rely solely on your vision. What you hear, for example, can help you keep moving away from or possibly around the threat. In hallways you need to check in front, but don't forget to protect your rear. Likewise, if you're using the stairs, you need to look down as well as up. In one instance, which I described in an earlier chapter, the victims came under fire as they exited a hotel room. They ran to the emergency exit and started down the stairs. The attackers knew they were unarmed and followed them. The victims beat their attackers to the street and were able to escape. Apparently the bad guys didn't mind shooting up the hotel but didn't wish to call attention to themselves on the street.

Another departure from the norm when implementing the "scan while moving" option is that, unless circumstances dictate otherwise, the handgun should not be displayed if you are armed. Here the snubby really comes into its own. You may have your hand on the gun in your pocket or shoulder bag. You may have a coat thrown over your arm and hand, concealing the gun. But unless you're a sworn peace officer in uniform or a plainclothes officer displaying your badge, you want to avoid being just another guy in civilian clothes waving a gun around in a pretty volatile situation! In the final analysis, the exit method you use may be pretty much self-selecting. If you're under fire or caught up by the crowd, you run. If the threat has not spotted you yet and the herd is starting to stomp their feet and mill around while waiting for the herd bull to tell them what to do, move so as not to draw attention to yourself.

If you are armed and circumstances force you to fire your weapon, you stand a good chance of being in a building full of people, many of whom you can't see, and many of whom may be in motion. Be sure of your target—what's in front of it, what's behind it (sound familiar?). Kneeling may give you a better angle with less chance of hitting an innocent party if your round(s) go through a wall. You want to be behind cover before firing. If you draw fire from the bad guys, you want to minimize the danger both to yourself and others around you. And again, especially in restaurants, don't forget the "+1" rule. There may be a backup shooter sitting at a nearby table sipping his or her ice tea when you go into action. Bummer. Especially if you forgot to get behind something.

And, finally, once you make it to the exit door, food for thought: Is your weapon concealed? Take a look outside and then walk out. If the cops are already in place and you come running out, gun in hand . . .

Training with the Snubby

WITH THE EMPHASIS ON THE PISTOL as the weapon of choice these days, it is tough to find anyone who offers a good training program for the snubby. Hopefully, that will change in the near future; until then we are pretty much on our own.

We need to consider not just training, but role-specific training for the short-barreled revolver. For instance, if you carry it as a primary sidearm, you will have one set of requirements, whereas if you carry it as a backup or second gun there are additional training concerns. Or perhaps you are not allowed to carry a concealed handgun in your city, but you have one for home defense. Your training should also take into account the fact that the snubby is at the low end of the power scale (depending on your choice of ammo), doesn't hold a lot of ammo, and can be a tough gun to shoot quickly and accurately in both the flea-weight versions and .357 Magnums carrying full-house loads.

Below I have outlined my ideas on training. It is solely a guideline and certainly not the gospel. For example, I think training with this gun should be conducted at ranges from 21 feet to contact, since that is where you are most likely to have to use it. Further, since the snubby might be called on in different locations, I would address this in the tactics for each level: Level 1 tactics would emphasize situations that might confront you on the street; Level 2 would deal with incidents that might confront you in your home; and Level 3 would focus on incidents that might take place when you are in or near your vehicle.

- *Level 1:* This is where you get those all-important basics, learning how to fire the revolver from the ready; how to draw and fire from a concealed carry; and how to reload quickly with a speedloader. Tactical training (street) would include moving with the handgun and identifying and using high and low cover. Proper mindset, situational awareness, and threat recognition and avoidance would be taught here as well as the legal requirements in your area regarding concealed carry, use of force, etc. Of course, handgun safety, proper gun handling skills, and how to clean the revolver are included. I would also introduce the use of OC spray here with scenarios on when to use the spray and when to use your handgun. Distances would be 3 yards to 7 yards and all firing would be two handed, eye level, with emphasis on the front sight.
- *Level 2:* Here the student is exposed to multiple targets. This places a real premium on good shot placement, since you may have as many as seven shots but more likely will have five or six. Firing with one hand only, the strong hand, would be covered prior to instruction on the use of the flashlight (both tactical and practical types) and low-light firing. Tactical training (home) would cover issues such as home storage of defensive firearms, fighting in your home with your family pre-

sent, the safe haven, holding a suspect at gunpoint, and how to handle yourself when the police arrive. Distances would be 3 yards to 7 yards, with emphasis on the front sight.

• *Level 3:* Here we deal exclusively with target-focus training, how to use the snubby without sights at eye level and techniques for firing when we can't bring the gun to eye level. The tactics (vehicle) deal with parking your car and approaching your car when you return to it, how to use your vehicle to get out of carjack situations, and when to drive and when to use your handgun. All training at this level is conducted at 3 yards to contact.

If you are new to handgun training the first three levels will probably suit your needs. If you carry the snubby as a backup you need Level 4. Students would have to demon strate handgun proficiency, safe gun handling and perform at an acceptable level in the scenario training before moving to this level.

• *Level 4:* In the first three levels we assume that the snubby is being carried as the primary sidearm, either by the lawfully armed citizen or by the off-duty police officer. In Level 4 we assume that it is being carried as a second or backup gun to a full-size service revolver or pistol. Here the student learns how to transition from the big gun to the little gun. He also learns when to transition. This is pretty obvious if his primary handgun is a revolver, but it is not always so obvious when his primary handgun is the pistol. Does the situation call for you to quickly reload, conduct a Phase 1 or Phase 2 malfunction drill, or scrap all of the above and go for the backup? Handgun retention is also taught. The student will learn how to use his backup handgun as a weapon retention tool. Where legal, he will also be taught how to use a knife as a weapon retention tool. Here we need to make it clear to the student that the police experience has taught us that if the bad guy gets your gun away from you he intends to shoot you. Weapons retention is a lethal-force encounter. Distances in this training are from 7 yards to contact.

All of this training could be squeezed into a week, but it would probably be better digested by the student in short sessions of, say, two and a half days each with some time in between each level for practice.

TRAIN SAFELY

All too often we read of training accidents in which a student is killed by a gun that shouldn't have been there. The excuses usually put forth are, in my view, almost as painful as the incidents themselves. In these days of rubber guns, Simunition, and Airsoft training technology, there is no excuse—none—for any student to be injured by live or blank ammo during training. We have to have a zero tolerance policy for this.

If you wish to dryfire ALONE in your home with an EMPTY handgun, by all means do so. And even though you are using an empty gun, Clyde Caceres tells me that he always advises his clients to have a safe backstop as another layer of safety. He suggests expired body armor for police officers, bookshelves, or possibly stacks of old phone books, anything that could stop a round from your handgun. However, the second that you introduce a partner into your training the real guns and real bullets need to be safely stored (unless you are live firing on a range, obviously). If there are no real guns and no live ammo involved when you train with a partner, you might still get hurt, but you won't get shot. If you are going to participate in Sims or Airsoft training, you should have a qualified instructor running the exercises, sufficient safety officers, and suitable safety gear.

But how about the preparation and practice phase, the training you do that prepares you to conduct an Airsoft

Crimson Trace's blue guns with Lasergrips are a superb,
safe training aid.

exercise? Or when you want to practice your ECQ drills
prior to going to the range? This is where the rubber gun
really comes into its own. You still have the heft and feel of
your carry sidearm, but you may safely point it at your
partner, confident that it won't go off accidentally. We've
had red guns for years.

But Crimson Trace has taken it one step further. By
adding a laser to a rubber gun, they have given us a really
versatile trainer that can be used in the classroom, hotel
room, vehicle, wherever, in complete safety. They have the
added benefit of letting you know whether you got the
technique right and if you "hit" your target, accidentally or
on purpose. Interestingly, as I talk to more and more people
about their impressions of Lasergrips, even those instructors who don't use them on their duty or personal carry

guns rave about the laser-equipped trainer they regularly use for training and practice. For all the gun-handling basics, such as drawing without "sweeping" yourself, practicing tactical training in use of cover or suspect control, disarming, backup gun drills, and so on, the CTC blue gun equipped with a laser can help you conduct training safely and effectively.

Without the laser the training can quickly become dull and repetitive. You can see students go through the motions, but there is probably very little learning or skill enhancement taking place. They may be getting sloppy and they may even be developing unsafe habits that will take their toll should they ever have to apply the drill for real. And while sometimes it is necessary to conduct firearms training and suspend the marksmanship requirement, we want to keep it to a minimum.

I think as instructors, we always prefer to conduct our training so that the student is constantly reminded of where his shots are going. The laser can do that for us. It keeps you honest while it keeps you safe. And if your carry handgun is equipped with Lasergrips, you are really going to maximize the time spent in training with the CTC blue gun.

ECQ Training
with the BUG

WHEN I'M TRYING TO EXPLAIN a particular subject, it always helps me if I understand the definition of it right from the start. ECQ, or extreme close-quarters combat, is a good example. What is it? How can I recognize it? What makes it different from CQC?

ECQ is a place you don't want to be. It is sometimes referred to as "The Hole," and that may be as good a definition as any. Technically, I think it is what is more commonly called in training circles the "Reactionary Gap," a distance that spans 6 feet to contact. It is within this distance that a good many gunfights take place. Within this distance you are more likely to be shot, cut, or punched before you can react because of the action vs. reaction times involved. You are real short of time in "The Hole." You are highly likely to have to use empty-hand techniques against your assailant before you are able to use your handgun. If your handgun malfunctions, you are not likely to have the time or the use of both hands in order to clear it. You are also real short on distance so your ability to apply tactics is virtually nonexistent. You will not have time to move to cover or gain distance. Indeed, your only choice may be to close the distance (attack!).

As I was putting this chapter together I called my mentor on such topics, Keith Jones. Jones is a Vietnam combat veteran, a serving police officer with more than 30 years on the street, and one of the most knowledgeable officer survival instructors that I know. He told me that, in his experience, you need to make sure people understand that if they find themselves in "The Hole," they're going to have to fight their way out, not shoot their way out. You are literally fighting with the handgun.

The fact that we address the unique requirements of extreme close-quarters fighting (with the handgun) in training these days is a good measure of how far we've come since I was in law enforcement in the '70s. In those days, the revolver was the issue sidearm for police, and the old timers would advise the rookie that he really should carry a second concealed handgun, just in case. For compatibility in training and on the street, it should probably be the same make as his duty revolver, and he should carry it so that it is available to his weak hand. Good advice then and good advice now, however, there endeth the lesson. I don't recall any agency providing training in the use of the backup gun. If there was any training it was for the off-duty revolver (same gun, different role). Even when weapons retention was recognized as an essential skill for the officer in the mid-'70s, it was all about fighting for the handgun, not fighting with it. And today, in spite of some earlier misgivings that I had, the snubby has come back as the solid favorite at all levels of law enforcement (federal, state, and local), as the backup gun of choice. We have almost arrived.

I say almost because we are not quite there yet. We have recognized the importance of the second, or backup, gun as an essential survival tool. We have recognized the need for extreme close-quarters training with the primary handgun. But from what I've been able to find in current training programs, including books and videos on the subject, we are still neglecting the backup revolver.

For example, all of the ECQ combatives drills I've seen are intended to allow the good guy to access his holstered primary handgun. So far, so good. But a fight, and especially one that turns deadly, is an unpredictable event. The only chance you have to deal with your assailant may come when your strong side or primary gun hand is not available. In a really bad scenario it may happen when your primary gun is not available. You are fighting for it, it is not working, or you have lost it in the fight. Consider the following:

Jim, a detective buddy of mine, and his partner go to a trailer home to serve a warrant. At the knock, the subject opens his door and permits them to enter. But as soon as they step into the trailer a fight breaks out, and my friend reaches for his handgun—a Colt .45 Gold Cup that he carries in a shoulder holster. As his hand wraps around the butt of the weapon, the bad guy grabs him in a bear hug, effectively trapping the .45 and Jim's hand between their bodies. (Jim tells me later that his left hand is free. Had he had a snubby in his pants pocket he could have easily gotten it into action.) Fortunately, Jim's partner pulls her trusty Colt Diamondback—the .38 Special version with the 2.5-inch barrel, certainly one of the handsomest and most accurate snubbies ever—and restores order to the fracas.

More recently, a U.S. Army NCO is involved in a hand-to-hand fight with an insurgent. The soldier has every intention of killing the enemy but, when the time comes, his hands are free, but his sheathed knife and his holstered pistol are sandwiched between them. Another young soldier saves the day.

There is another issue to consider here regarding the use of the primary handgun in ECQ techniques. These days your primary handgun will most likely be a pistol and, from what I've seen in several ECQ training videos, there is a lot of emphasis on how to draw the handgun to a retention position as part of the firing stroke when you are struggling with your assailant. Fine, but what if you need to fire, but you can't create the required space with your handgun crushed against your assailant? Most pistols are likely to only offer you a single shot. Some, like the Colt 1911, will not fire at all if the slide is forced out of battery by sufficient pressure on the muzzle. Keith Jones told me that some of his officers prefer the small pistol to the small revolver for a backup; however, they soon learn (with deactivated training pistols) that if they carry the handgun in their left-hand pants pocket and end up on the ground, and especially if they roll over, they stand a good chance of depressing the magazine release, rendering the pistol a single shot unless it has a magazine safety, in which case it won't fire at all.

And there is also the Mother Nature factor. Drawing and bringing your handgun to a retention position before firing in an ECQ drill is good training and makes sense. I'm just not sure if it will be there for us in a lethal encounter when we are in physical contact with our assailant. I think our tendency (instinctive?) is likely to be to shove the muzzle of our handgun against our assailant before firing.

In this book I describe an incident in which this happens with an officer who is being choked to death. Marshall and Sanow document this response in the "Street Results" section of their books on handgun stopping power (available from Paladin Press). Whether your attacker is in front of you or behind you, we see the same thing: You are in a fight for your life. You have one chance to take an action that will save your life. You can't see your handgun. You know that you don't want to miss and you don't want to shoot yourself. You jam the short barrel of your revolver into your assailant and pull the trigger. You continue pulling the trigger until the fight stops. We can argue that possibly your training will override this apparently instinctive reaction. However, much as we have learned over time in our study of close-range confrontations common to the handgun, Mama Nature may make the dedicated Weaver shooter use the isosceles. It may force the confirmed sighted-fire shooter to use target-focus techniques. Consider the following account, which is probably one of the best descriptions we have of what can happen in an extreme close quarters lethal encounter.

• • •

In 1976 the San Diego Police Department, in conjunction with the U.S. Border Patrol, formed the Border Crime Task Force, a 10-man decoy unit that patrolled the "no-man's land" between Tijuana, Mexico, and San Diego, California. The officers dressed, talked and acted like the illegals who were coming across the border. They were armed with standard department-issued Smith and Wesson Chiefs Special revolvers and at least one team member carried a High Standard 12-guage semiauto shotgun under his coat. They were supposed to cut down on the violent crime that was a nightly occurrence on the United States side of the border in this area of just a few square miles. Joseph Wambaugh wrote a book entitled *Lines and Shadows* (a Perigord Press publication) that documents the 18-month history of this unit. What follows is just one of their many violent confrontations that Wambaugh describes in this book with the detail of a seasoned police investigator. (The officers involved here are Manny Lopez, Tony Puente, Joe Vasquez, Joe Castillo and Carlos Chacon. They are about to confront three bandits in the dark.)

Tony Puente decided to move a few steps to get between the nearest bandit and the border.

The bandit perhaps didn't like him moving, because it happened. Very very fast. The bandit lunged for Tony Puente. He grabbed Tony and Tony grabbed him. Then everyone made his move.

Joe Vasquez had been told earlier that if he ever had to drop someone quick without the bandit's motor reflexes coming into play, he had to take off the back of his head.

Joe Vasquez in that microsecond saw something that Tony Puente did not see. And Vasquez jumped on the back of the bandit who had grabbed Tony Puente. In this bizarre nightmare instant the young men embraced in a three-way bear-hug dance, in the moonlight, on the edge of the precipice.

... Joe Vasquez broke the bear hug long enough to place his two-inch .38 up against the back of the skull of the bandit and ...

It was unquestionably the loudest explosion Tony Puente had ever heard. ... The round was fired in his face. His eyes were burned by the muzzle flash and stung by lead shavings. He was blinded.

... The greatest shock of all was experienced by Tony Puente ... one of the embracers suddenly let go and the world's most gigantic explosion went off in the face of Tony Puente, and his polka partner dropped his head on Tony's shoulder like the sophomore at a prom and his brain fluid started gumming up and welling down his neck ...

Tony started yelling at Joe Vasquez, "Joe, you killed the guy. He wasn't hurting me, Joe! ... Why did you shoot him?" Joe replied, "Tony, he was trying to stab you!" "I didn't see any knife," Tony said.

Joe Vasquez pointed under the body of the bandit... and there it was. A long blade with the handle wrapped in tape. A stabbing knife.

• • •

So here we have yet another example of the muzzle being jammed against an assailant or "stapling" as Jones calls it. And we have an officer who couldn't see a deadly threat because he was being crushed against his assailant. Two officers at contact distance with a bad guy but both have a totally different view of what is going on. I think this is a really graphic example of where ECQ training needs to start. Take away the officer who actually shot the bandit. You are now on your own, struggling with an assailant in the dark in terrain that allows for very poor footing, your partners are engaged with other bandits and you don't know if this guy is armed or not. So you can't shoot him, yet ...

As you can see there is, quite literally, more to ECQ training than meets the eye. And we are only addressing one piece of it, the backup gun. The point we want to make is that you need to be able to finish the fight with either hand. That is one of the reasons to carry a backup gun. Probably the best way I can put this into perspective for you is to again draw on Jones' hard-earned wisdom. In his weapon retention classes he has found over the years that the student can stay in the fight at full capacity for about 30 seconds. He teaches them a really simple technique that allows them to stay on their feet, protect/retain their primary sidearm, and go for a backup handgun or knife. He finds the average time it takes the student to access his backup weapon and get it into action is about four seconds. The students tell him that the technique is great and it works, but the real bonus is the confidence it gives them. They know that if someone attempts to disarm them they will have a conditioned response on tap that will quickly allow them to effectively deal with the bad guy or "change his channel" as Jones likes to say.

And finally, Jones told me that he finds that the big advantage to ECQ training in general, and the weapon retention training in particular, is that it makes his students aggressively possessive of their Reactionary Gap, making it hard for someone on the street to get close to them. He makes them believers in the fact that it is easier to *stay* out of "The Hole" than it is to *fight* your way out.

Carjacking
Countermeasures

I INCLUDE THE USE OF THE VEHICLE under available tactical options because, while it is relatively easy to find information on when to use your OC spray or unarmed skills instead of the gun, it is not so easy to find such information on when to use the vehicle as a means of allowing you to escape safely from a situation instead of using your gun.

So in this chapter I take into account the fact that, as a private citizen, you are going to find the courts will look upon you more favorably if you can demonstrate that you did everything you could to get away from the threat. I hope also to clarify when to use the handgun, when to drive, or when to simply let the perpetrator have the car. As a general rule, if you are in the car and the threat is outside the car, if you have room to maneuver, and your car is running, then the car becomes your preferred response option. Simply by stepping on the skinny little pedal on the right, you can extract yourself from a good many problem situations.

Carjacking, then, is the taking of a vehicle by force, or the threat of force, while the victim is in or around the vehicle. The information that I have was taken from the Bureau of Justice report *Carjacking in the United States, 1992–1996*. This study identified the following carjack characteristics:

- They usually involved a single victim
- The carjacker's weapon of choice was a handgun
- The carjacker's second choice was a knife
- Most carjackings occurred within five miles of the victim's home
- They took place on a public street near a bus, subway, or train station
- They took place in parking lots or near stores, restaurants, gas stations, and office buildings

As we note in the definition, a carjacking may take place when you are near or at, but not in, your car. So carjacking presents you with a twofold attack recognition issue. The first is recognizing a problem when you are not in the car but either walking up to it or standing beside it. The carjacker may approach you and ask a question before making his move. He may take advantage of the fact that you are preoccupied with putting the groceries in the car or getting the kids strapped in. He may hide in a van parked next to your car. So during your approach to the car you need to be practicing your "avoidance through awareness" skills. Pay attention to what is going on around you. Pay particular attention to what is happening in your 21-foot/360-degree safety bubble and use large doses of common sense. Situational awareness is the key here.

If you are in the car, you are at risk when the car is not moving, so you need to be especially watchful at stop signs and stoplights. Anyone who approaches your vehicle while it is stopped is automatically suspect. They may approach from the front, sides, or rear, so you need to constantly be using your inside/outside rearview mirrors. Watch their hands, look for weapons and have your escape route picked out, when possible. This is why you always want to travel with the doors locked and the windows up. This is the reason you always want to be able to see the tires of the vehicle in front of you when you are stopped in traffic for whatever reason. This gives you the room to maneuver. Be prepared to run over a curb or even leave the roadway for a short distance if you have to.

Variations on the theme may be for the carjackers to follow you home, block you with their car in your driveway, and take your car. Or the "bump and rob" in which you are rear-ended at a traffic light. When you get out to inspect the damage they grab your car. If you are rear-ended, before doing anything, look in the rear view mirror. If there is only one person in the car behind you it may have been an accident. If there are two or more people in the car, it may not have been an accident. Consider the possibility that one of them may be about to become the proud new owner of your car and proceed to a safe haven before getting out of your vehicle to exchange insurance info.

I have been involved with evasive driving technique from both an operational and a training perspective since the late 1970s. I have had the opportunity to become very familiar with these skills overseas in countries with all of the crime issues any big city faces, often with a significant terrorist threat thrown in as well. My experiences and observations have convinced me that, in the United States, if you have a couple of years of driving experience under your belt, especially in a major urban environment, you already have sufficient driving skill to get out of the vehicle crime scenarios you are likely to encounter. What usually jams the untrained driver up in a carjack attempt is not driving ability—the skill that is missing is attack recognition. If you don't see it coming or you can't recognize what is happening, and if you have no conditioned response available, sheer luck can only do so much. (Police officers, protective operations specialists, and those whose work requires them to live abroad will require some additional training.)

• • •

Following my retirement from the government, I worked for a time for a company that taught kidnap avoidance skills—including evasive and offensive driving—to businessmen in Latin America. This incident was related to me by one of our students, a corporate executive in Mexico.

His story begins one day when he comes home from work and pulls into his driveway. He is accosted by two local policemen who relieve him, at gunpoint, of his watch and wallet. They do this in front of the executive's young son, who is in the car with him at the time. Since he couldn't go to the police with his problem, he takes it upon himself to ensure that if there ever was a next time, he would have some options. He ordered an evasive driving film from a mail order firm in the United States called Paladin Press.

Luckily or unluckily, it turns out, there was a next time. He was taking his date home at about 3 am. There was no traffic on the road and he was driving in the left lane. On his left was the median, lined with trees and with a high curb. A late model car pulled in front of him.

The executive noticed that the license plate was dangling from the rear of the car. It was apparently loosely tied with string. Just about the time it took for him to notice this and wonder about whether the car was stolen or not, a second vehicle pulled up on his right side.

Then, several things happened simultaneously. The car in front of him started to slow down as the passenger in the rear seat of the vehicle to his right produced a gun. My friend screams at his date to get down as he panic breaks, slams the car into reverse and mashes the accelerator. He told me that he kept the car in reverse until he was sure they weren't chasing him. Then he turned his car around and ducked down a side street. With no training except a video, he did what he thought would work, something he was used to doing every day, although certainly not at speed! He backed up and then, when he felt safe in doing so, he turned his car around.

His ability to perform some simple driving maneuvers helped him get away from the threat. But what saved the day was his situational awareness and attack recognition. Thus, the attack did not take him by surprise and he was able to instantly react.

• • •

As with any motor skill, the ability to "do the necessary" during a critical incident requires a combination of soft skill/hard skill training. Soft skills include situational awareness, the survivor's attitude, route analysis, surveillance awareness, and attack recognition. Hard skills are the driving responses you apply when you must take action to avoid, evade and/or counter a particular threat. The soft skills plus attack recognition scenarios are what you mostly pay for in evasive driving instruction. The actual driving is just fine-tuning skills you already possess.

Since the current crop of vehicles most people drive these days can only do three things (go-stop-turn), your evasive responses are going to have to be pretty straightforward (no pun intended). During my government service I had access to virtually all incidents involving foreign service personnel, and I was able to debrief some of them regarding the details of what actually took place. My study of incidents in which evasive driving techniques have been used successfully revealed the following were used pretty much in order:

1. Just step on the gas. If there is nothing blocking your vehicle's forward progress, this is as simple as it gets. Head for the nearest safe haven (police station, fire station, shopping mall, anyplace with lots of lights and lots of people) and tell someone you had a problem.
2. If someone is blocking your forward progress simply drive around them. This is why you need to be able to see the rear tires of the car in front of you when you are stopped.
3. If your forward progress is completely blocked, go backward. As with the incident I related above, go backward until you no longer feel threatened, then turn the car around and head for the nearest safe haven.

• • •

The chauffeur for a wealthy Latin American businessman was taking the children to school in an armored vehicle. As he approached an intersection, a car shot out from a side street and blocked his forward progress. He noted that two armed men got out of the car and started walking back toward him. Without warning, they began firing. As they got to the side of the car, still firing, the driver noted that one man even changed handguns. Suddenly a round penetrated the armored window, striking the chauffeur in the arm. The impact snapped him out of his shock and amazement, and he slammed the car in reverse and backed up until he could no longer see the men. He then turned the car around and sped back to the family's residence.

• • •

Note that all of the vehicle responses involve taking decisive action and either getting the car in motion or keeping the car moving. This gets you away from the attack site. It also provides you with another big plus—you now become a lightly armored moving target. Not only are you harder to hit because you are moving and presenting an ever smaller target, but the more distance you can put between your vehicle and the shooter, the tougher it is for his rounds (especially handgun bullets) to penetrate the body, or metal "skin," of your vehicle and reach the interior of the car. The bullet can still get through the glass, but it just can't get a good "bite" on the moving car body. We can say that an armored car that does not move may be at greater risk of bullet penetration than the unarmored car that speeds away. An armored car that is sitting still runs the risk of rounds "woodpeckering" their way into the car, which is exactly what happened in this case.

And what about the fancy stuff, the J-turns and bootlegger spins? They are a waste of valuable training time. Another lesson I learned from my study of actual incidents is that no one uses them in the real world! When someone is trying to carjack, kidnap, or kill you, simple is better. I think, for whatever reasons, trainers tend to put vehicle critical incidents (you have a car, they have a gun and maybe a car as well) into a different category than firearms critical incidents (you have a gun, they have a gun). For some mysterious reason we seem to expect the student to be able to perform complex motor skill activities with a vehicle, but we pride ourselves for teaching stress-proof technique with a firearm. It's almost like we believe that survival stress and its complications won't happen to the driver in a vehicle critical incident; therefore, we tend not to select out evasive driving techniques requiring complex motor skills in favor of something more practical. That is why we saw people in real situations simply do a "U" turn (which they had not been taught to do) instead of the more complex technique requiring independent hand and foot coordination (which they had been taught to do). Yet another reminder that training that is not designed around critical incident realities, both human and tactical, will not serve us well.

I suspect also that is one of the reasons ramming was so successful; you can keep going forward while knocking the other vehicle out of the way. One of the benefits of training in how to ram another vehicle is the realization that it is pretty difficult for a single car to block your way. We also found that ramming is like riding a bicycle; once you learn it you never forget. The longest time I was able to document between taking the training and then having to apply the skill—a situation in which one of our operations officers had to ram another vehicle to escape—was seven years.

So keep in mind that whether you are inside or outside your vehicle, you need to pay attention to what is going on around you in order to Detect-Assess-Avoid-Evade-Counter-Escape Safely. If your assessment tells you that you cannot Avoid-Evade-Counter, then giving up the vehicle may be the safest thing for you to do.

But what if you have small children in the car, strapped into their car seats? How do you give up the car but not them? The carjacker is probably scared, paranoid, and likely to be under the influence of alcohol and/or narcotics. In short, he's wired ... and he probably has a gun.

- Do not make any sudden moves
- Tell him he can have the car
- Tell him you are unbuckling your seatbelt
- Speak firmly and decisively but don't shout
- Tell him you are taking the children with you—do not ask his permission
- Get the kids and walk away, go to the nearest safe haven
- Contact the police

Now it gets complicated. What if the person forces you into the car or gets into the car with you? You really do not want to stay in the car with the carjacker, because you are now facing grave personal risk. There are any number of reasons for his wanting you to accompany him, and none of them are good. So if you are outside of your car when the carjacker makes his intentions clear, or if he gets into the car with you after doing so, the gun now becomes an option. As we frequently hear in training classes, "Just because he has a gun doesn't mean he's going to use it. Just because he shoots at you doesn't mean he is going to hit you. And just because he hits you, it doesn't mean you're going to die."

• • •

The woman had been visiting a friend at the hospital. She walked to her car in the parking lot, opened the passenger door, crawled across the front seat, and unlocked the driver's door from the inside. She then got out and walked around to the driver's door and opened it. "I simply have to get that lock fixed," she thought as she slid behind the steering wheel. She was startled by the realization that there was a young man seated next to her holding a gun. He had gotten into the car in the time it had taken her to walk from the passenger's side around to the driver's side. They drove aimlessly for about 15 minutes and then he ordered her to drive him down a dirt road. Instinctively, she knew that her assailant had just made a decision that placed her in mortal danger. She had a .38 Special snub-nose revolver in her purse, which was on the floor of the car between the seats. She made the decision to go for the gun. Surprisingly, she was able to pull it out of her purse before her assailant could react, and she was struggling to pull the trigger when he shot her and fled. Seems a well-meaning family member had purchased a holster for the handgun as a surprise for her and forgot to mention it. Thus, she was unable to get her finger on the trigger. She survived the wound.

• • •

The off-duty cop suddenly realized that the man seated next to him in the front seat was going to kill him and take his car. Both of the cop's hands were on the steering wheel. The man across from him held what looked like a

.25 auto, but it was getting bigger by the second. The officer did not know what kind of gun the man in the backseat had. The two had flagged the officer down, told him they had car trouble, and asked if he would take them to a filling station. Once the two got into the car, the guns came out. The off-duty cop had three things working for him: These guys weren't likely to shoot him until they got off of the busy street they were on; they didn't know he was a cop; and they didn't know he was armed. He decided to go for it. With a draw that would have made the Guinness Book, he produced the Chiefs Special and, just as quickly, emptied it ... three at the assailant next to him and two at the one in back. The carjacker in the front seat died where he sat. The one in back escaped into the crowd with a shattered left thumb.

• • •

These are examples of "The Hole," which we discussed in an earlier chapter. Once again, this situation probably bears no resemblance to anything you have ever done in training. Can you execute a disarm from a sitting position? Can you block his gun hand while you draw your weapon as a brother officer did in an incident we described above? Can you imagine yourself drawing against two armed men in the confines of your vehicle? Could the lady have simply opened her car door in the parking lot and run away? Is there anything we could have done to avoid this in the first place? These are situations in which you decide that if you do nothing you are very possibly going to end up worse off than whatever might happen to you if you fight back.

As I was finishing this chapter, a young college student was the victim of an attempted carjacking in our state capitol. According to the news report, she was stopped at a red light at about 2:00 in the morning. A male subject attempted to open the door and get into the car. She stepped on the gas and ran the light. He fired a single shot that went through the rear window of the vehicle and grazed her arm. She drove until she was able to alert a police officer, who escorted her to her parent's home.

Are You
Ready? Part II

I AM ALWAYS LOOKING FOR INCIDENTS in which the handgun is used. During a conversation with Michael DeBethencourt, president of the Northeastern Tactical School, he introduced me to two books that are must-read if you own a firearm for personal protection. They are *The Best Defense* and *Guns Save Lives* by Robert A. Waters. In his books, Waters provides us with detailed true accounts of situations where armed citizens used firearms to protect themselves and their families. The attacks he describes are in many cases as physically brutal and tactically complex as anything a police officer might face.

After reading these books, I decided to answer some of my own questions. To the books I added my old copy of *The Armed Citizen*, an NRA publication that contains extracts from the column of the same name that appears in various

NRA magazines. I also found a few incidents in Jack Lott's book, *More Guns, Less Crime.* This gave me accounts of incidents involving armed citizens that roughly spanned a period from 1958 to 2002.

The approach I took while reading these accounts was to take standard handgun range training and compare it to what took place during the incident.

For many people, the only formal training they will receive on the handgun is what they are required to successfully undergo for their concealed-carry permit. For an even larger number of people, those who choose to keep a handgun in the home, there may be no formal training at all. They will learn what they learn from friends and relatives, television, and the movies, and maybe books and videos. Some may have some familiarization with the handgun from their military service. With rare exceptions the handgun skill levels of the people in these accounts is minimal. I could not document a single instance in which anyone had attended one of the "name" schools such as Thunder Ranch or Gunsite. Despite their lack of formal training (but more importantly, in my opinion) they all possessed in large quantities something we can't teach—that indomitable spirit, the will to survive, the inner strength that allows you to stand toe-to-toe with a bigger and stronger assailant, and whoever else he brought to the fight, trade them blow for blow and shot for shot and defeat them! I am reminded of Kipling's timeless advice in *If.*

> *If you can force your heart and nerve and sinew*
> *To serve your turn long after they are gone,*
> *And so hold on when there is nothing in you*
> *Except the Will which says to them: "Hold on!"*

We all know what goes into an introductory handgun program for permit applicants. In addition to the classroom time there will be the basics of how to load and fire your handgun, usually based on how you need to do it in order to meet the requirements for the qualification course. You'll likely practice in presenting the handgun from the ready and drawing it from the holster. Most everything will be done in the standing position. The use of the front sight will be emphasized. Maybe use of cover will be practiced. And there will be a session on low-light firing and use of the flashlight, holding a suspect at gunpoint, and dealing with the police who respond to your 911 call.

When I looked at actual incidents, this is what I found:

• The attack will happen very quickly. It will leave the victim little to no time to react. If you are given a danger sign or two and you miss them, you'll start way behind the power curve. The danger signs were usually visible (how a person was acting, where and how they were positioned) or audible (sounds of a door being kicked in or the voice of a family member or coworker who was obviously in distress).

• The bad guys might point their guns at the intended victim or threaten him with a knife to get him to comply with their demands. Or they may immediately attack the victim by beating, shooting, or cutting and stabbing him. (So you are already injured, hurting, and confused when you decide to fight back.) The attack can be vicious beyond your comprehension of what one human being can inflict on another. Worse, if the attack takes place in your home the beatings, knifings, or sexual assault may go on for hours because there is often little risk of discovery.

• The only thing that stopped the attacks were firearms in the hands of determined individuals willing to use them. (Note: I'm sure you are all aware that on more than a few occasions the mere display of a firearm was sufficient to stop a situation from escalating; however, in many of the cases I looked at, the firearm wasn't available to the victim prior to the assault. It was not on their person when the attack began.) Storeowners frequently kept a handgun at the register. Homeowners had them in a variety of locations, usually the bedroom. Long story short, they had to fight their way to the gun. There were several specific comments about the various gun- or trigger-locking devices, none favorable. They felt the devices were an unnecessary complication when you needed the handgun in a hurry. It was noted in one case that during an incident, a homeowner had to remove a trigger lock before she could use her firearm. According to Waters, when the individual purchased a new firearm after the incident the first thing she did was to throw the trigger lock away.

- The victim's weapon of choice was usually a small handgun. The most frequently used handgun in the 44-year period I looked at was the .32 revolver. Other popular calibers were .22, .25, and .38 Special.

- Unfortunately, ammo type was rarely documented. Shot placement was sometimes good, sometimes poor, and sometimes not reported. What was clearly evident, however, was that regardless of bullet type or shot placement, even in the few instances where a shotgun was used, nothing seemed to take effect very quickly. In many of the cases described, the fight continued even after the attacker was hit multiple times. Sometimes he ran out of the place of business or residence and collapsed from his wounds. In other cases he made it to a hospital or was dropped off there by his confederates. Waters attributes much of the failure-to-stop problem to the fact that many of the attackers were under the influence of crack cocaine.

- Frequently, there was more than one attacker. This was the rule rather than the exception.

- Distances were not documented, but from reading the sequence of events and looking at the location (in the room of a home, at the counter of a business, while seated in a vehicle) it would appear that many of these very violent actions took place from 5 feet to contact or grappling distance. With an exception or two, a shot taken at between 5–10 feet was a long one.

- The use of sights was not documented, but the distances involved, the often desperate struggles that were taking place, and the comments some of the victims made afterward suggests that sights were seldom used. The victims were watching the actions of their attackers and not the front sight. ("I didn't see any bullet holes." "I didn't see any blood." "I thought I'd missed." "It wasn't like you see on TV where they slam backwards and fall.")

- I could only find one instance where the victim reloaded. While there were plenty of cases in which more ammo would have been helpful, that's not the way it happened.

- There were a number of situations in which a family member was either being held at gunpoint or was fighting with one of the attackers when another family member with a gun had to shoot.

- The victim was usually standing, sometimes struggling with an attacker, when he fired his handgun. In some cases the victim was on the floor before he was able to shoot. This was either as part of getting to the firearm or as a result of being knocked down by his attackers. It appeared that the storeowner, if prone, was most likely to be on his stomach while the homeowner was often on his back (in bed). The carjack victim was obviously most likely to be seated when he or she began firing.

- There were a disturbing number of these incidents where the victim was tied or taped up and had to free himself before he could get to a gun and deal with his attackers.

Well, as usual, in the end it's always the questions that are easy and the answers that are tough. Has your training prepared you to deal with the kinds of assaults these people faced? Are you ready?

Robert A. Waters
P.O. Box 771509
Ocala, FL 34477
www.robertwaters.net

Michael De Bethencourt
Northeastern Tactical Schools
P.O. Box 591
Nutting, MA 01865

PART

SOMETHING OLD,
SOMETHING NEW

The Bulldog: A Faithful Companion

WHEN PALADIN PRESS DID THE SECOND printing of *The Snubby Revolver*, they changed the cover. The new cover sports a .45 Colt New Service "Fitz Special," which was presented to Colonel Rex Applegate by J.H. Fitzgerald. You can see the inscription on the revolver's sideplate that reads, "To Rex From Fitz." Given my immense respect for the Colonel's many contributions to what we now call CQC, I am honored to have this particular revolver on the book's cover. Was this the same "Fitz Special" Applegate carried during the six weeks he served as a bodyguard for President Roosevelt during WWII? And how would the story have read if Applegate had been carrying this revolver instead of the .38 S&W he used during that shooting incident down in old Mexico? We're talking some pretty serious history here.

As a result of this I decided to take a look at the revolver variant known as the Bulldog, past and present. By definition the Bulldog is a big bore, short-barreled revolver. However, I plan to take some liberties with this definition as I discuss some of my favorites. As near as I can tell, the prototype for the Bulldog was the Royal Irish Constabulary (RIC) revolver made by Webley. It came in several calibers, but the most common one was the .455 Webley.

The U.S. counterpart to the RIC Bulldog was the brainchild of J.H. Fitzgerald, who headed the testing department of Colt firearms for many years. His "Fitz Specials" were made from the Colt Police Positive Special in .38 Special and the .45 Colt New Service. His customizing included cutting away the front of the trigger guard, removing the hammer spur, cutting the barrel back to 2 inches, shortening the ejector rod, and rounding the butt of the revolver. He also slicked up the action.

We know that the .45-caliber "Fitz Special" was a favorite of several professionals who carried a handgun as a necessary tool of their trade. In addition to Applegate, Fairbairn and Sykes, of Shanghai police and OSS training fame, liked the cutdown revolver. While both men were confirmed 1911 advocates for uniformed carry, they stated their preference for the .45 snubby for the plainclothes officer for its quick draw, first shot capability at close quarters.

During some of his Border Patrol adventures, Colonel Charles Askins carried a Fitz copy made up by his good friend George Parker. And at least one New York City police detective carried a cutdown .45 Colt that I personally like the looks of better than the "Fitz Special." It is probably, to my eyes anyway, the most purposeful looking defensive firearm I have ever seen. Someone did a really nice job on that gun and you may have seen the photo of it in Chic Gaylord's book, *Handgunner's Guide.*

As best I know, we probably didn't have a commercially available Bulldog until Charter Arms brought out their .44 Special in the early 1970s. I owned two of the stainless versions, one in 3-inch and the other a 2 1/2-inch. I went totally Charter for several years and carried the 2 1/2-inch

Bulldog with the little Charter .38 Special snubby as back-up. They both came with dehorned hammers and excellent fixed sights. I carried the 200-grain Silvertip hollowpoint in the Bulldog. I liked the gun and I liked the company. Charter Arms had a very good customer service department and they were always most helpful. As I was overseas during this time, I really appreciated their cheerful assistance.

The big problem I had in those days with the Bulldog was spare ammo. This really bothered me because one of the advantages of that big bore is that the cylinder also has big charge holes; it is a breeze to reload in a hurry. The only speedloaders available at the time wouldn't reliably hold five rounds. I bought several from different stores and they all had the same problem. Since I carried the Bulldog concealed, the speedloader went into a pocket. At best I could only count on four rounds when I reached for the speed-loader, which did not make me a happy camper.

This was in the late 1980s and, while I was pondering this problem, Ruger introduced the SP-101 in .357 Magnum. It was available from the factory with a spurless hammer. While the .357 snubby may not be a true Bulldog by definition, I'll offer that it is certainly one in terms of performance. I found that the speedloaders for the "pocket rocket" worked just fine and rode handily in a pocket. And so began my conversion to the .357 snubby as my primary carry gun.

Up to this time a short-barreled wheelgun, especially on the Chiefs Special frame, was a .38 Special. In a six-shot frame we had some dandy .357s with barrel lengths from 2 3/4- to 2-inches. These were the Ruger Speed-Six, the Model 19 S&W 2 1/2-inch and the Colt Lawman in 2-inches. I had a real soft spot for the Speed-Six with a spurless hammer and used one as a trainer during my police years. The Colt Lawman and later the .357 Detective Special, the Magnum Carry, were probably the closest Colt ever came to offering a modern day "Fitz Special." Interestingly, while the Speed-Six, the Lawman, and the Magnum Carry are no longer made, true Bulldogs in .44 and .45 bore are more available today than ever before and .357 snubbies have become quite popular.

The true test of anything, especially when it comes to firearms, is how well it does overtime. Guns designed for the street will be looked at with an especially critical eye. The criteria by which they will be judged may vary a little depending on whether the handgun is to be carried concealed or on a uniform duty belt, but we can rest assured that the evaluation will be uncompromising. The Bulldog concept is as valid today as it was a century ago. We recognized then and we recognize now that if you're carrying something small and concealable, with a limited ammo supply, should you need to use the gun it had better hit with authority.

The same can certainly be said of books. They may entertain, they may educate, or they may do both. Or, as we know, they may do neither. Some will have lasting appeal and some will be very short-lived. They will withstand the test of time or they will not. In my own case, thanks to you, this book is in its third printing. The copy you now hold in your hands is updated and expanded. I will be most honored if you should judge *The Snubby Revolver* by its cover.

Remember the Six-Shot Snubby?

SINCE THIS BOOK IS ABOUT the snubby, I thought I'd best wrap up with a chapter on the subject. It didn't seem like that long ago when we were debating the merits of the five-shot revolver vs. those of the six-shot revolver. Today, however, I feel like I'm writing a historical footnote. Two separate events forced me to give this issue some thought. The first was Colt's decision to stop production of the faithful Detective Special just about the time they got it right with such options as dehorned hammers, rust-resistant finishes, a front-sight-only night sight (my favorite), a smooth action, and a .357 Magnum version, which was long overdue.

The second was a class Mike Boyle, a senior official in the New Jersey Department of Natural Resources and well-known gun scribe, offered at the 2000 Tampa International Association of Law Enforcment Firearms Instructors (IALEFI) entitled "Back to the Future: Snub Revolver for Pistoleros." I was unable to attend the class, but Mike recently mailed me a copy of his lesson outline, and it was chock full of useful, practical information on the short-barreled revolver. But the real point I need to make here is that hardly anyone attended Mike's class, which leads me to conclude that even the five-shot revolver's role as a backup handgun is rapidly becoming a thing of the past in law enforcement. I know that before I retired from federal service a number of government law enforcement agencies specifically prohibited their agents from carrying the little revolver as a backup weapon.

All of which leads me to further conclude that the snub-nose revolver market will soon be the exclusive domain of the private citizen, if it isn't already. Interesting. Certainly not something I would ever have considered seeing in my lifetime.

The good news is that the snubby is alive and well these days in more flavors of five-shooters than ever before. Smith & Wesson, Ruger, and Taurus offer something for everyone in a variety of calibers and weights. With space-age metals, these companies have developed revolvers that weigh about as much as a cylinder full of the ammo they carry! We may have just about perfected the design of a handgun intended to be "often carried but seldom shot." It is not too much of a speculative leap to entertain the idea that this may in fact be the new role of the .38 Special revolver, since hardly anyone is using the 4-inch-barreled version anymore.

As I pondered what all of this meant, it dawned on me that not having the Detective Special in the marketplace has severely reduced the availability of the six-shot revolver. To my way of thinking, this is not a good thing. Much as I love the five-shot, it is at its best in a backup role to a bigger gun. This was well known in police circles back when the revolver ruled. In fact, it gave rise to the (old) Conventional Wisdom (CW) that you shouldn't carry the five-shot 2-inch as your primary sidearm. Although plainclothes officers and off-duty cops frequently ignored this advice, it was reality based. It was recognition of the fact that an all-steel (20- to 21-ounce) five-shot snubby stoked with +P .38 Special ammo is right at the ragged edge of what most of us can control in rapid-burst firing.

This advice did not apply to the six-shot snubby. Why? The most obvious answer is that it gave you another round. True, but not the right answer. The strong suit of the six-shot snubby is that it is generally easier to shoot quickly and accurately than the five-shot version. The six-shot tends to give you a "fistful of gun." This pretty clearly defined the roles (old CW) of the two revolvers as: five-shot (backup) and six-shot (as the primary gun or if you are only carrying one gun). As a further example, if you have ever had the opportunity to see both guns at work on the range, you probably noted that while those using the five-shot had to really work to qualify, their comrades armed with the six-shot 2-inch shot about as well as they did with the 4-inch service revolver. The all-steel Chiefs Special weighs about the same as the all-steel Detective Special, but the slightly larger Colt gives you more gun to hang onto. More to the point, several officers I knew who were in shootouts with a Chiefs Special upgraded their choice of weapon. Not so with the six-shooters. They never seemed to suffer from performance anxiety before or after.

So much for the old CW. Today's (new) CW tells us that the first rule of gunfight survival is: *Always have a gun.* The gun manufacturers have taken away the weight factor as an excuse. Since most situations involving the lawfully armed private citizen are close-range affairs that are usually turned off by the display of a handgun, you are still on pretty solid ground with almost any type of small pistol or revolver.

The problems start if you have to take it to the next level, if you are forced to shoot. With practice, most people can manage the recoil generated by +P .38 Special loads in all-steel snubby revolvers. But if you choose to go below 20 ounces and carry the airweight or titanium guns, recoil becomes grim. Practice with these flea weights is more important but less likely than with the heavier versions. They hurt! I know that you will probably not notice the recoil if you are forced to fire during an armed confrontation, but the laws of physics will still apply.

One suggestion may be to buy the lightweight to carry and the all-steel version to practice with. Since all of this is about the ultimate concealed-carry handgun and what we are looking for is something that packs like a Seecamp .32 but packs a wallop like a .357 Sig, we need to consider some possible compromises, which leads to my second suggestion. I'm as enamored with those gorgeous lightweights as the next person. For me, the midsize (six-shot) airweights have been a solution at times. During my law enforcement days, the off-duty gun I eventually settled on was a 2-inch S&W Model 12, the lightweight version of the Model 10. With a set of Herrett's Detective Grips, it was a shootin' machine. I found it much more controllable in rapid fire than my Model 60 Chiefs Special, and it carried effortlessly in a Don Hume IWB holster. Those favoring the Colt were quite happy with the lightweight six-shot Agent. (Although no longer offered by S&W or Colt, these slick little revolvers are fairly easy to find in gun shops and gun shows.)

Of course, the real solution is that someone needs to bring back the genuine article. Actually, the Colt Magnum Carry would be a good place to start if anyone were to ask me. My friends are all hoping this will happen soon. They're getting real tired of my drinking their beer and asking the inevitable question, "Does anybody remember the six-shot snubby?"

The Saga Continues

LITTLE DID I KNOW WHEN I started this book with a story about DEA and revolvers that I'd be ending it with a story about DEA and revolvers. One of my old DEA colleagues told me about this incident, and when he learned I was writing a book about the snubby, he mailed me the related newspaper clippings. In truth, I could not have found a better example of the little five-shot in action. But more to the point, as you shall see, it is people, not guns, who win gunfights.

The following is a paraphrased version of a 31 December 2000 report in the *Chicago Sun-Times* (written about two weeks after the shooting, when the details became clearer).

• • •

It was the day after Chicago was hit with a foot of snow. Trains were running late, and crowds were milling about Union Station throughout the day. A DEA agent was working special detail with an Amtrak investigator and a Chicago police officer when they became suspicious of two Amtrak passengers.

The team agreed to approach the men (Daniel Wentworth and Andrew Ross) and question them after they stepped off in Chicago around 1 P.M. for a layover.

The DEA agent approached Wentworth when he walked into the station concourse. Wentworth began to open his jacket, revealing a pistol and alarming the Amtrak investigator and the police officer standing a few feet away.

"Gun!" the Amtrak investigator yelled.

The Amtrak investigator and the Chicago officers grappled with Wentworth and wrestled him to the ground. Wentworth pressed a .40-caliber Glock to the back of the police officer's head as the Amtrak investigator held the muzzle of the gun, sources said.

"Back off, or I will blow her f——— head off!" Wentworth allegedly said.

The police officer managed to hit a button that ejected Wentworth's ammunition clip, leaving only one bullet in the chamber, sources said.

As his friend struggled on the floor, Ross pulled his own Glock and scuffled with the DEA agent . . .

• • •

Chicago Tribune (14 December 2000):

A federal agent emptied his five-shot revolver at one suspect in Tuesday's shootout at Chicago's Union Station, picked up that man's gun after he fell wounded to the floor, and then shot and killed a second suspect who had a weapon pointed at another officer, law enforcement sources said Wednesday.

• • •

Chicago Sun-Times (14 December 2000):
In the deadly gun battle at Union Station, a federal drug agent faced the situation of a lifetime. His five-shot pistol was out of bullets after he had wounded one gunman, but just feet away, a second gunman had a .40-caliber Glock trained at the head of a Chicago police officer. The quick-thinking federal agent grabbed the gun of the wounded man and used it to shoot and kill the second gunman, authorities said Wednesday.

• • •

Portland Press Herald (15 December 2000):
. . . A DEA agent emptied his five-shot revolver into him [Wentworth], then used Wentworth's gun to kill Ross, who authorities say was holding the gun to the head of the Chicago police officer. It was all over in a few seconds.

• • •

All of the news accounts agree that the two bad guys were both wearing body armor and were armed with .40-caliber Glocks and an undisclosed number of spare magazines. Obviously, they had considered the possibility of a shootout. And yet neither of them fired a shot, even though at one point during the confrontation they had their guns drawn and pointed at the officers. We might say that they were prepared but they weren't willing. Not so the DEA agent, whose intensive training gave him the mind-set and the skills to do what needed to be done. As I read through the details of how this gunfight unfolded, I couldn't help but think that it could serve as a veritable checklist for Jeff Cooper's *Principles of Personal Defense*.

And so the five-shot snubby continues to write its own impressive history. For many of us, it is the bottom line in defensive handgun selection. It is the perfect combination of size, weight, power, concealability, and reliability. Street tough and combat proven. As I write this, it is comforting to know that the saga of the snubby continues.

• • •

S&W OK'D FOR DHS/ICE

On January 4, 2006, officials at Smith & Wesson issued the following press release, entitled, *Smith & Wesson Models Authorized by Department of Homeland Security for Personally Owned Weapons Program.*

Springfield, Mass., Jan. 4 /PRNewswire-FirstCall/ — Smith & Wesson Holding Corp. (Amex: SWB), parent company of Smith & Wesson Corp., the legendary, 153-year-old, global provider of products and services for safety, security, protection and sport, announced today that the U.S. Immigration and Customs Enforcement (ICE), the largest investigative arm of the Department of Homeland Security (DHS), has authorized ten Smith & Wesson revolver models for inclusion in the Personally Owned Weapons Program.

The newly established Personally Owned Weapons Program allows DHS and ICE agents and officers to purchase and carry personally owned firearms for on-duty and off-duty use. Currently, ten Smith & Wesson revolver models are included on the list of firearms from which approximately 10,000 agents and officers will be authorized to purchase and carry.

"Through our partnership with the Department of Homeland Security, we have been able to further establish ourselves as a key supplier of high quality firearms and services to the military, to federal law enforcement agencies and to the federal government," said Leland Nichols, Smith & Wesson's vice President of Sales. "The Personally Owned Weapons Program allows agents to select firearms based on their individual preferences, while ensuring a level of quality and reliability for each firearm. We look forward to working with the DHS, its agents and officers in this and other capacities."

A wide selection of Smith & Wesson J-frame revolvers is included on the list of authorized Personally Owned Weapons Program firearms. The ten revolvers include a diverse mix of stainless steel, scandium alloy, carbon steel, titanium, and aluminum alloy components. Revolvers from Smith & Wesson's Airlite® Series, Airweight® Series and Chiefs Special Series are represented on the list. Authorized revolvers on the list include: the Model 340PD, Model 342, Model 36LS, Model 360PD, Model 37, Model 442, Model 60LS, Model 637 and Model 642LS.

About the Author

ED LOVETTE is a retired CIA paramilitary operations officer. He was also a captain in the U.S. Army Special Forces and is a 10-year law enforcement veteran. He has a long association with *Combat Handguns* magazine for which he currently writes the "Survival Savvy" column. He and his wife live in Laurinburg, North Carolina, with their two dogs and the occasional houseful of grandkids.